MW01268425

Four Levels of Meaning in the York Cycle of Mystery Plays

FOUR LEVELS OF MEANING IN THE YORK CYCLE OF MYSTERY PLAYS

A Study in Medieval Allegory

Jefferey H. Taylor

The Edwin Mellen Press
Lewiston•Queenston•Lampeter

Library of Congress Cataloging-in-Publication Data

Taylor, Jefferey H.
   Four levels of meaning in the York cycle of mystery plays : a study in Medieval
allegory / by Jefferey H. Taylor.
       p. cm.
   Includes bibliographical references and index.
   ISBN-13: 978-0-7734-5578-8
   ISBN-10: 0-7734-5578-7
   I. Title.

hors série.

A CIP catalog record for this book is available from the British Library.

The Edwin Mellen Press   The Edwin Mellen Press
Box 450   Box 67
Lewiston, New York   Queenston, Ontario
USA 14092-0450   CANADA L0S 1L0

The Edwin Mellen Press, Ltd.
Lampeter, Ceredigion, Wales
UNITED KINGDOM SA48 8LT

Printed in the United States of America

Dedicated to my parents: Mennell Harvey Taylor, Sr & Velma Whetten Taylor

Lo debido a los padres jamás está pagado—
Sin embargo una pieza os he entregado.

Table of Contents

Foreword by Alexandra Olsen   i

Acknowledgments   iii

Introduction   1
Localizing and Generalizing in Cultural Discourse

Chapter 1   11
The Audience and Culture of the York Cycle

Chapter 2   29
Typology and Boethian Time in the Structure of the York Cycle

Chapter 3   49
Fifteenth-century Mystical Nominalism in the York Cycle

Chapter 4   79
Ritual Compensations

Notes   97

Bibliography   103

Index   113

Foreword

The York mystery plays, forty-eight pageants covering sacred history from the creation of the world to the last judgment, are known from a single manuscript (dating from around 1463-1477), now in the British Library. Traditionally, the plays were presented on the feast day of Corpus Christi, a movable feast occurring the Thursday after Trinity Sunday, between May 23 and June 24. A great deal of information exists about the staging of the York plays, which were probably first presented in 1376 (the year that the existence of pageant wagons is recorded in York) and were banned in 1568. Each play was subsidized and presented by members of a particular craft guild ("mystery" means "craft" in Middle English). The cycle uses twenty different verse forms and was probably written by several anonymous clerics, one of whom is conventionally called the "York Realist." Since most literature composed in the Middle Ages was aimed at the elite class, the Corpus Christi plays are noteworthy because they were written for a wider audience. It is known that Queen Margaret saw the plays performed at Coventry in 1457, but the York plays are obviously intended for an audience which included the average citizens of York.

The critical understanding of the Corpus Christi plays inherited from the nineteenth century suggests that they were composed by learned clerics for an uneducated audience but do not reflect learned clerical values. This understanding has been reinforced by some recent critics, who view the plays as folk literature and deny that there was any connection between scholasticism and folk art. In the present study, Jefferey H. Taylor has written a major reconsideration of the York plays, arguing that they show a sophisticated use of Boethius's theories about time. He argues that the discussion about whether the plays were produced by clerics or truly represent folk literature is irrelevant because clerics and the common people did not inhabit completely separate worlds but shared a common world view. Critics who believe that the plays were not written by clerics tend to argue that the plays must be naïve productions and cannot include allegorical elements. In contrast, Taylor suggests that the structure of the York Cycle with its pattern of Fall and Redemption, best seen in the Pilate play, indicates that it was written with a nominalist epistemology that must have been understood by the entire audience. The world view of the plays presents ideas found in the philosophical works of the late Middle Ages.

As a result of the misunderstanding of the intellectual milieu of the Corpus Christi drama, the critical history of the York cycle as well as all the other English Corpus Christi plays has been one of condescension and scorn, viewing them as artistically deficient because their episodic structure comprised of a series of discrete events is different from the structure of modern drama. In recent years, critics have produced more subtle readings of the plays, seeing unity of purpose in their juxtaposition of the sacred and the comic. Taylor has written a major study which argues that Medieval allegory with its four levels of meaning (literal, typological, tropological, and anagogical) was part of the epistemology of all members of the audience. He argues that typology, which holds a place of special importance in Medieval literature, informs the structure of the York cycle and that its study leads to a reevaluation of the audience of the York plays, showing that fairly sophisticated allegory was understood by all members of the audience. As a result, Taylor argues, a richer cultural milieu was available to the common people than has traditionally been assumed, and they were capable of understanding the epistemology of symbol and mediation. In the York plays, Christ's intervention in history is typological but cannot be understood without the tropological intervention of the Holy Spirit in individuals (seen for example in the Pentecost play), and the anagogical level, which represents the union of the soul with God, best seen in the Last Judgment. The plays thus present a communal and anagogical experience, in line with Pope Urban IV's bull of 1264 and 1311 establishing the feast of Corpus Christi.

Alexandra H. Olsen
Professor of English
University of Denver

Acknowledgments

I offer thanks to the many people who have helped me, directly and indirectly, with this project. My gratitude to scholars and mentors who helped in the early phases of this work: Thomas J. Hatton, Margaret Winters, Paul Olson and William J. Brown. Two professors set me on this path many years ago: Roberta Bosse and Stella Revard. Many thanks to the members of Bede and Beyond, the Denver area Medieval Studies group, who patiently listened to drafts of chapters and offered pertinent critique and moral support, especially Alexandra Olsen, Elizabeth Holtze, Chuck Carlson, Roberta Payne, Pam Troyer, Diana Williams, and others who share the camaraderie of the group. I offer gratitude to many scholars who helped in simple ways, including the many members of the Perform email listserv and my colleagues at Metropolitan State College of Denver, especially Rudy García for helpful conversations, and Cynthia Kuhn, who offered encouragement and advice. Richard Beadle kindly gave permission to quote from his edition of *The York Plays*. Thanks also to Richard Collier for permission to quote from his seminal book, *Poetry and Drama in the York Corpus Christi Play*. AMS Press was prompt and helpful in acknowledging the fair use of material from Clifford Davidson's *From Creation to Doom*. Special thanks to National Library of The Netherlands (Koninklijke Bibliotheek, Nationale bibliotheek van Nederland) for permission to use the picture of the Last Judgment on the front cover, taken from manuscript The Hague, KB, 71 G 53.

I thank my parents, Harvey and Velma Taylor, who have encouraged my study of culture and literature throughout my life and have given me multicultural perspectives that I could not have received from anyone else. My children, Melian and Andrew, have been patient, loving and supportive. Most particularly, I thank my wife, Leslie A. Taylor, whose insights, encouragement and scholarly expertise have been a constant source of inspiration and guidance.

Introduction:
Localizing and Generalizing in Cultural Discourse

In the past two decades the "academic conversation" about Medieval drama and culture increasingly has become focused on particulars of local material culture. This thickening of description, prescribed by anthropological theorists such as Clifford Geertz and Mary Douglas and finding its execution in various New Historicist methods, has done much to develop a richer view of Medieval life, resisting the stereotypes of previous scholarship. An admirable example is Gail McMurray Gibson's *The Theater of Devotion*. Yet one of the reasons Gibson's work is so effective is that she does not allow her careful, thick description of local culture to preclude connections with broader cultural movements: she finds resonance between East Anglian religious life and that of Flanders and Germany instead of "the previous century's court poets" and "the Italy of Dante and Boccaccio" (4), and in her chapter on the Cult of the Virgin she rightly finds that the Marian devotion "we associate today with Italy and Spain [. . .] was in the Middle Ages of English renown" (138). The problem, then, with earlier cultural analysis was not that it dared draw broad cultural links but that it began from unexamined assumptions.

Thickening and localizing description prove to be important critical tools, but to the extent that the localizing of cultural discourse renders anathema any attempt to grasp the larger scene of culture, it has the potential to subvert the very program of the humanities it seeks to enrich. If we are to interpret culture, we must risk broad observations, despite the perils of cultural relativism. In *Local Knowledge* Geertz warns:

> But a serious effort to define ourselves by locating ourselves among different others [. . .] involves quite genuine perils, not the least of which are intellectual entropy and moral paralysis. (234)

Nonetheless, he argues, we cannot escape these difficulties:

> The double perception that ours is but one voice among many and that, as it is the only one we have, we must needs speak with it, is very difficult to maintain. . . . But however that may be, there is, so it seems to me, no choice. (234)

Douglas takes this challenge head on, exploding the stereotypes inherent in social analysis exactly by pursuing a typology (in the modern sense of the word) that insists that localized perception is circumscribed by generalized boundaries:

> Yet something about institutional forms is generated by elementary choices and the resultant institutions incorporate judgments which reciprocally influence further perceptions of choice. Once any one of those elementary choices has been made, it entails a package of intricately related preferences and secondary moral judgments. . . . If the swirling movements of individual choices were entirely haphazard, all institutions would long ago have become more and more alike. There would be no scope for recognizable typology. ("Grid/Group" 5-6)

Indeed, when observing another culture, though we must admit the epistemological limitations inherent in our contextual perspective, we undoubtedly draw conclusions based on the relative consubstantiality, to borrow Kenneth Burke's terminology, between our context and the one we are observing. For Douglas, there is more cosmology inherent in the implicit, the unspoken assumptions of discourse, than in material culture (*Implicit* 3-4). Localizing culture, thickening description, can greatly empower our ability to perceive the ambience of other cosmologies, but only if we are brave enough to attempt to develop and critique typologies (in the modern sense) that help define relative perspectives. Douglas writes:

> A famous social psychologist, when I mentioned the word typology, shrank in dismay. He sought to defend methodological purity against my concern to make sense of the larger scene. Typologies, he said, allow anything to be fitted into their boxes; they become an over-powerful interpretative tool. Wondering how one is even to make the smallest progress without developing any typology, I could have quoted from Katrina McLeod the Confucian rebuke to those who shirk their obligations in the name of purity. . . . If we eschew explicit typologies which can be

criticized and improved, we may stay in a celestial harmony and escape from having to deal with the relation between mind and society, but the cost of our private purity is to expose the whole domain to undeclared, implicit typologies. Either way, behavior is going to be fitted into boxes. (Douglas, "Grid/Group" 2)

Much of the current conversation about Medieval culture has insisted on the impossibility or undesirability of any attempt to "make sense of the larger scene," to pronounce upon generalities which inevitably function to inscribe differences between our implicit cosmologies and those of older times and other places. In response, Margreta de Grazia in "World Pictures, Modern Periods, and the Early Stage" interrogates the post-modern critique of "world pictures" as a construct of modern critics without reference to earlier times by suggesting that the prevailing ideologies of modern criticism themselves function as representational mediations similar to the traditional ideas of "world picture" they attempt to refute (8). Her article helps to clarify both the dangers and inevitabilities of modern circumscriptions of perspective, suggesting the inescapable relevance of "historical pictures."

> [A] World picture or period concept or ideology may be less a methodological convenience than an epistemological necessity. Without such an act of enframing, the past would appear either a massive monolith or as myriad details. In addition, it would blur into the present. Once bounds are drawn, however, a historical object can emerge. Putting a frame around a temporal span is what enables us to see something inside it. It is the very condition of visibility or intelligibility. . . . (8-9)

This resonates well with Lee Patterson's critique of New Historicism that "historical criticism must abandon the hope of any theoretical foundation and come to rest instead upon its own historically contingent moment" (250-1). This, however, does not render moot the very program of cultural criticism, but rather recognizes our limitations in a productive way. In a bold challenge parallel to Geertz's, Patterson concludes: "While this may indeed seem a distressingly unstable basis for historical knowledge, I would ask the reader to reflect upon the possibilities of any other" (251). We cannot escape the uncomfortable need to view the past through our own eyes and mark significant differences. Certainly,

4

generalities always hold weaknesses, most apparent when applied too widely, capriciously, or without reference to present cultural motivations. Yet we cannot escape essential perceptions of difference between ourselves and our Medieval forbearers, and some of these differences undoubtedly cross lines of locality, class, gender, nationality, and several generations. The problems of perception cannot be cured by refusing the task; rather, as Douglas suggests, we must mark our cultural framings clearly so that they are open to criticism and improvement. Yet Douglas's recognition of the structure inherent in social cosmology suggests that the attitudes of de Grazia and Patterson (and Geertz) need not be seen as settling for limits to perception or leading to a nihilistic defeatism; rather, culture itself frames these referents as people continually create it. Perception of the past, then, is not radically different from perceiving the so-called present. Further, the limits of social cosmology as defined by Douglas's Grid/Group matrix and the tensions between the extreme ends of the matrix offer the hope that we might indeed be able to perceive essentials of past cultures in productively adequate ways. Literary texts in particular offer much that reflects social cosmology. It may be helpful to "strange" the interpretation of literary texts with other cultural artifacts, but all one has to do is examine past cultures from which we have no texts to be reminded of the incredible power of texts and stories to illuminate culture.

I suspect that much of the dominance of focused, localized criticism and the rejection of any attempt at generalities arise at least partly from the circumscribed social cosmologies of modern academia. James M. Jaspers in a recent essay in *The Chronicle of Higher Education* entitled "How the Research-University Model Has Killed the Creativity of Humanists and Social Scientists" laments the dissolution of the original aims of the humanities and social sciences through the increasingly tortuous application of the "naturalist" research model requiring hyperspecialization and science-like data sets and eschewing any attempt to do what the humanities do best—paint broad pictures of culture and social change.

> What does the naturalist model imply for those in the social sciences and humanities, however? Here, hyperspecialization can be the death not only of creativity but of solid understanding, for it is often the big picture that is most important. (Jaspers)

The demands of the tenure system's love affair with this naturalist model are most damaging for humanities scholars:

> Many humanists will resist, drawn by the equally powerful image of liberal education. Unfortunately, they will continue to suffer for their resistance. They must choose between wisdom and career success. (Jaspers)

Not surprisingly, the increased difficulty of upholding this model in our competitive times, decried by Stephen Greenblatt in the role of MLA chief, has only exacerbated the problem. A recent report in the *MLA Newsletter* confirms that rather than heeding Greenblatt's call to reconsider tenure requirements, most humanities departments are toughening their demands for rigorous, specialized publication (Scholes 3). This fits well into the predictions of Douglas's Grid / Group cosmology. As cosmologies fail, the natural tendency is to reinforce the very cosmological model that is leading to failure, hence the down-grid spiral of highly competitive Low Grid / Low Group societies such as ours (Douglas, "Cultural" 239). Academia is not immune to these dynamics. The humanities have suffered greatly from this movement into increasingly difficult competition in hyperspecialization.

To bring this line of thinking back to the problem with the present conversation about Medieval drama and culture, we need only look at lost lines of inquiry in the field. One example is the impact of philosophical nominalism on late Medieval literature and culture. Just as Indiana University was finishing, at long last, the dissemination of the writings of Charles Sanders Peirce, most theorists in the history of ideas dropped any conversation connecting Medieval philosophy with common culture, and, of course, its connection with modern Anglo-American pragmatism. The 150 year obscurity of much of Peirce's writing led most historians of philosophy to conclude that Peirce was influenced mainly by Duns Scotus and Kant in developing pragmatism.[1] The publication in 1982 of Volume 2 of *Writings of Charles Sanders Peirce* showed that Peirce saw his pragmatism as an extension of the critical nominalism of Ockham and others, and, further, that he saw nominalism as the defining factor in English thought preceding and following Ockham for many centuries: "The most striking characteristic of British thinkers is their nominalist tendency. This has always

6

been and is now very marked" (Peirce 310). Presently any attempt to use nominalist thought to illuminate the differences between Medieval and later culture is likely to be rebuffed by arguments that no link can or ought to be found between isolated scholarship and localized public culture. Yet, this assumes that nominalism was strictly a product of the isolated academy rather than perceiving that Ockham was himself a product of and embedded in his culture. Compare this assumption with David Knowles's contention that Ockham's "name and his works became famous because they exactly suited the temper of and the tendencies of his age" (327). Some scholars perhaps fear that any reference to formalized philosophy would inherently subsume the culture to the philosophy instead of the philosophy to the culture.

A related line of thinking seemingly lost in the race to reject traditional delineations of history and culture is the almost wholesale abandonment of the use of allegorical typology to examine the workings of late Medieval societies just at the time when all the pieces needed to synthesize that understanding were in place. An argument against linking supposedly esoteric scholasticism with popular culture merely echoes the original antagonist position of critics such as E. Talbot Donaldson and William Manly that assumes the common people were unable to understand the complexities of patristic allegory, arguing that it was an isolated exegesis of the elites. Again, this assumes that these scholastic theories did not arise from the culture, but rather were mere aberrations of thought unconnected with any local cosmology. Opposed to this contention are the arguments of critics such as R. E. Kaske and Walter E. Meyers that grant a greater coherence to Medieval societies and a richer cultural milieu to the common classes. Unfortunately, it would seem that a revival of this debate was not actually pursued; the topic was merely dropped along with most generalizing conversation.

There is, of course, risk inherent in any attempt to define other cultures through one's own, as Geertz has warned, including opening oneself to the perennial accusation of arrogance or lack of qualifications to paint with a broad brush. But unless we take these risks, we risk a worse fate: reducing the humanities to specialized trivialities. We must heed Jaspers's warning and attempt to interpret in interpretive fields, developing typologies (in the modern sense) of social cosmologies that localize by reference to broader social structures.

Ironically, the desire to drop all attempts at generalizing statements about culture lends credence to the notion that common peoples exist in a cultureless void of basic human responses, an idea thoroughly discredited by the very anthropological theories that inform the new localizing criticism. Generalizing discourse on historical periods and culture does not necessarily preclude the life of the individual or obscure the continuing social struggle over meaning. Patterson's critique of the anti-individualism of New Historicism (263-7) is similar to Douglas's critique of traditional sociology. One of the great powers of Douglas's Grid / Group matrix of social cosmology is that it resists the static idealism (and resulting ethnocentricities) of earlier sociologies by asserting that cosmology is constantly being negotiated by individuals in their daily social transactions (Douglas, "Cultural" 189-90). Similarly, Erik Paul Weissengruber's analysis of processional conflict in Medieval York calls for "a sociology of symbolic struggle" that would "better assist historians in investigating how rituals functioned in York's social space" (136). Was not some of that symbolic struggle framed in the allegory? And was this epistemological framing a mere academic aberration or a common folk inheritance? At the least I would assert that an epistemology of symbol and mediation was generally operative among a broad range of Medieval peoples. Allegory might achieve sophistication in limited circles but it was nonetheless an essential part of the basic epistemology of the culture. Yet, if the popular drama is any indication of popular culture, then it would appear that some fairly sophisticated allegory was commonly understood by many people in late Medieval England. We can find coherence in past cultures without mocking them or blinding ourselves.

Almost fifty years ago Northrop Frye suggested that the Cycle drama's presentation of well known, significant mythology was "designed to remind the audience of their communal possession of the myth" (282). In a much overlooked article, Kevin Roddy extended Frye's suggestion positing that the Cycle drama contained qualities similar to epic poetry and functioned to "affirm [the] collective belief" of the audience, creating "a communion with the divine will" (158). Though the "collective belief" was undoubtedly not as monolithic as these statements might sound, there certainly was a "collective belief" that gave coherence to the culture so that even those such as the Lollards who objected to the prevailing orthodoxy are defined by their objections, not by an entirely different set of beliefs. Hans-Jurgen Diller in a recent article, "Laughter in Medieval English Drama: A Critique of Modernizing and Historical Analysis," contests the Bakhtinite views of critics such as Anthony Gash, hinting at the potentially ridiculous assumptions of positing acute rifts in the culture of late Medieval York by pointing out the wide conspiracy that an extreme, anti-orthodox reading of the Cycle drama would entail, a conspiracy implicating most of the society, including the authors, directors, actors and audience of the drama (6-7). Such a wide conspiracy goes by the very name of culture! That social cosmology is being contested in public performance does not preclude cultural coherence. On the contrary, if Mary Douglas is correct in her analysis, such symbolic struggle is a sign of cultural authenticity not of a fractured cosmology or epistemological nihilism.

We must, then, press forward with the program of cultural interpretation and, while not ignoring the limitations of epistemology, neither can we allow those limitation to preclude the process. In that spirit, the time is ripe for a long awaited synthesis of typological criticism, especially as applied to the Mystery Cycles of late Medieval England, a synthesis that offers much toward the program of "making sense of the larger scene" of the late Medieval world. The workings of typology inherent in the structure of the York plays cast light on the implicit cosmology of the people who produced them, watched them, even those who objected to them. Using the literary text itself to frame the context for such an investigation is not inherently tautological. Patterson aptly puts the literary text at the center of cultural analysis:

> These texts can hardly tell us everything we want or need to know about the past, but when securely located at the center of our investigations [. . .] they can help us to negotiate an otherwise enigmatic terrain. (270)

I believe this is unnecessarily understated. Texts are our best keys to culture with much to tell us about the on-going negotiation of social cosmologies.

Picking up the dropped threads of the debate over allegorical typology, a debate seemingly won by those who favored its ability to enlighten our view of

Medieval societies, I wish to both synthesize the argument and extend it. If we can allow allegorical typology in criticism, then we might investigate whether other levels of allegory are also part of the cultural fabric. Further, if we can demonstrate that these scholastic notions reflect prevailing attitudes, rather than residing in some culturally unconnected scholastic void, we open up the possibilities for re-examining other ideas, such as nominalism, that, though they seem esoteric to modern critics, may have much bearing on the life of individual persons and communities, local and transnational, in the period under question.

My purpose is to examine Medieval allegory with its four levels of meaning (literal, typological, tropological, and anagogical) not as an exegetical tool only for scholars but as a part of the epistemology of a broad set of societies interrelated in time and place in such a way that they collectively offer a coherence that may be distinguished from other times and places, giving rise to the desire to assign potentially useful labels such as 'Fifteenth-century York,' or 'Medieval Western Europe.' I wish to show how the complex varieties of 'knowing' found in these levels of meaning are implied by the structure and message of the York cycle of mystery plays. My purpose is to reveal broad perspectives of late Medieval English culture and how the culture is evoked by these plays.

In the first chapter I review how the study of typology in Medieval drama during the period from the 1950s to the early 1990s leads to a re-evaluation of the Medieval audience. The audience of the York cycle must have been a culturally informed audience for whom the sacred knowledge conveyed by the plays was primarily evocative rather than didactic. On the literal level, the audience experience reflected, reinforced—and sometimes contested—a commonly held cosmology.

In Chapter Two I find the cosmological structures that give rise to typology implied in the structure of the plays. The Boethian Time / Eternity contrast at the heart of Medieval cosmology is represented in the plays by a structure in which discrete episodes of mortal history are vertically linked by a framework that begins and ends in Eternity.

In dealing with the tropological level in Chapter Three, I find a nominalist epistemology implied in the Fall and Redemption argument of the whole cycle. Free will and divine purpose co-exist from a perspective in which human action is indeed free, but entirely meaningless in the divine scheme of things except when it conforms to God's purposes. This solution follows the logic of Ockham's critical nominalism as extended in the fifteenth century into cultural productions such as the mystical nominalism of Nicholas of Cusa and the Flemish painters' use of verisimilitude.

In Chapter Four I examine the anagoge created by the experience of the cycle, exploring the ritual level of Medieval York's self-defining discourse. The perspective of history afforded by the cycle is God's perspective, creating a ritual identification with deity carefully focused by the frequent inclusion of the audience in the action. The cycle's ritual power compensates for the limitations of human experience and knowledge, specifically the human inability to directly possess the experience of God's Eternity and the experiences of the cultural past, the central sources of contemporary cultural meanings. This difficult mimetic struggle parallels our own perennial struggle to interpret the past through the lens of present contexts.

My desire in pursuing this program of cultural interpretation is to identify the systems of cultural knowledge implied by the representations in this most complete of mystery cycles. The York cycle is an evocative representation of local cosmology, with inescapable implications for a broader analysis of societies interrelated in time and space. The recovery of the audience and the recovery of the meaning of the text cannot be separated. The best key to understanding the cultural view of the audience, whatever thickening of context that specialized analysis can add, is contained within the work itself, a work that functioned in its time as a ritual construction of social cosmology.

Chapter 1
The Audience and Culture of the York Cycle

Despite the conclusions of culturally based criticism in the past few decades, the Medieval Mystery plays are still often characterized as didactic productions from clerical sources meant to impose culture and values on illiterate commoners. For example, Oxford's new edition of the *Medieval English Literature* anthology published in 2002 characterizes the cycle dramas as "holy and didactic," devised by the clergy to instruct "the ordinary Christian" about "current religious belief" and "moral teaching" (Trapp et. al. 461). Such discourse implies that cosmology is socially imposed from the top down, divorcing the common classes from any cultural production, reinforcing the elitist notion that common people do not have culture, that culture is not a social product but a political imposition. This notion about culture resonates with the 19th century elitist view of Matthew Arnold and ignores the implications of current theory in anthropology and criticism. An examination of the language of the two opening plays of the York Corpus Christi Cycle reveals the evocative and performative nature of these plays, a nature inherently antithetical to a primarily didactic function. This, in turn, implies that the audience was a culturally informed audience for whom the structures and symbols of the plays were easily identifiable and highly communicative.

The legitimizing of typological criticism for Medieval drama studies in the latter decades of the 20th century has led to a reevaluation of how common Medieval people perceived their world. Since Auerbach's "Figura," the study of typology has been used by many critics to construct readings of Medieval texts— extensivley so in the study of the Mystery cycles. The greatest strength of such an approach lies in its attempt to recover what literature and art meant to Medieval audiences. In such criticism the recovery of meaning in literary texts necessarily involves the recovery of their cultural contexts. Questions of audience perception are especially important when examining drama because dramatic performance implies an audience—in this case, the citizens of York over a period of several centuries.

Typology studies sometimes have come under fire because they imply that familiarity with typological significance was available to the audience— something many critics have argued is unreasonable due to the audience's supposed lack of sophistication. The argument that "sophisticated" exegesis cannot be used to interpret popular drama, that the audience of Mystery cycles was not culturally informed, can be used to eliminate many similar cultural tools from the legitimate arsenal of the critic. The question then arises: What cultural knowledge did Medieval playgoers possess? We might also ask: On what level of audience sophistication should we judge the art of the plays? And, what level of cultural sophistication is needed to understand concepts such as typological significance? Indeed, these questions lead us straight to the heart of a culturally based criticism. The legitimizing of the use of typology in the study of popular drama supposes an audience whose perspective is culturally informed and clearly embedded in the cosmological contexts of the society. If we can demonstrate this informed perspective for typology then we can extend these arguments to the other levels of Medieval allegory and to other cultural tools of interpretation, such as traditional iconography, popular philosophy, theology, and so on. The text of the York cycle itself should offer the best evidence for a culturally informed audience perspective, for if the audience was culturally embedded and informed, then the narrative style of the text must be evocative rather than didactic.

I. Typology and the Interpretation of Medieval Culture

Most critical views of typological readings of the Mystery plays are directed by what the critics believe about the audiences' abilities to understand and recognize typological pairings and their significance. These run the gamut from Arnold Williams and William Manly who doubt that the audiences could perceive much from any typological (or any other) connections in the plays, to Pamela Sheingorn and Richard Homan, who see the average Medieval playgoer as steeped in the traditional significances of typology and iconography. The one side of the argument assumes cultural ignorance on the part of most Medieval people; the other grants to them a rich cultural superdialect of symbols and ideas. Inevitably, these schools of thought define 'typology' very differently. For the one, it is an esoteric exegetical tool for the privileged few; for the other, typology is a central tenet of Medieval culture and thought. The latter argument has been strengthened by the critique of traditional, "Auerbachian" typology offered by Richard K. Emmerson in "*Figura* and the Medieval Typological Imagination." However, to understand this insightful redefining of typology, we must review the development of the two opposing arguments with their opposing definitions of typology.

In the late 1960s and early 1970s the argument over whether typology was useful or not as a critical tool peaked with the opposing views of Arnold Williams and Walter Meyers. In 1967 Lawrence Ross had set the stage for the critical conflict by re-examining the question of the thematic unity of the Wakefield *Second Shepherd's Play* in his article "Symbol and Structure in the *Secunda Pastorum*." The conventional view of earlier critics such as A. P. Rossiter was that the Mystery dramas were disjointed hodge-podge works with little of the artistic balance found in the art of high culture. Ross pitted Manly's argument that rural audiences would not have seen the connection of the Mak scenes in the *Secunda Pastorum* with the conventional ending, against Margery Morgan's point that the audience knew the story well enough to make the connection obvious.

Ross pointed out that the opinions of Rossiter and others are colored by the traditional insistence that the Medieval dramatic structure was the torn and clumsy duality of vulgar, undeveloped secular farce patched into sacred ceremony. Ross suggested that our modern ignorance of the modes of representation available to Medieval dramatists and audiences hinders us from distinguishing dualities from unities in Medieval drama, while the concept of irony developed in the sixteenth and later centuries actually encourages us to see dualities where Medieval audiences saw unities (178-180). He argues that the understanding needed to see the connection between the two parts of the *Secunda Pastorum* was generally available to all Medieval playgoers, and that the unity of Medieval mystery drama can be seen through the Medieval view in which all things physical are metaphors of the spiritual (198-9).

This set the stage for the polarizing of critical attitudes toward typology. Arnold Williams resorted to the Rossiteresque argument that Medieval audiences were too vulgar to create or to know true art and declared the use of typology in criticism to be a fashionable fad originated by misapplied methods. In response, Walter Meyers, perhaps from Ross's lead, certainly from Auerbach's, argued that Medieval culture was filled with interrelated meanings that unified its cosmology, the most important element of which was typology and its peculiar historical focus.

The polarized differences in social cosmology between Modern and Medieval societies undoubtedly shape some of the debate over the perception of allegorical meanings. These differences can be mapped using Mary Douglas's Grid/Group theory of social cosmology, outlined in the essay "Cultural Bias" (190-208). Modern Western societies tend toward the Low Grid – Low Group corner of the matrix (quadrant A); hierarchical societies are in the opposite quadrant (C), High Grid – High Group. A society's social cosmology tends to be supported by a concomitant epistemology. In High Grid societies, traditional cultural meanings are favored over a negotiated epistemology, sometimes even to the point of adherence to customary meanings against obvious reason. In Low Grid, we favor an epistemology of rational argument, all meanings being potentially negotiable at any time, sometimes even to the point of a sophistry that ignores all semantics. As a result, Modern, Low Grid people tend to mistrust highly symbolic communications such as allegory and therefore have difficulty believing in their epistemological efficacy and widespread recognition. However, in High Grid – High Group societies, traditional, communal symbolism, strengthened by the enshrining of hierarchy and group, may easily serve as a cultural superdialect, widely accepted and implicitly understood by the general populace. Indeed, one of the greatest difficulties we have in examining all aspects of Medieval cultures is our tendency to submerge insulation and group, the very qualities that Medieval social cosmology enshrines.

Beginning with Morgan's objection that Medieval audiences would know the story of the Shepherds too well to miss the links between Mak's thievery and the birth of Jesus, critics who have wanted to use typological arguments have continually and increasingly granted knowledge to the masses of Medieval peoples that earlier critics claimed they could not have possessed. Meyers in response to Williams has offered evidence from many popular sermons and popular religious poetry to demonstrate that typological significance was an idea generally available to the Medieval world. Later critics continued to confirm this direction of thought. In 1987 Martin Stevens affirmed Meyers' view that typology was not erudite in the Middle Ages and, though confessing to be an admirer of Arnold Williams, objected to the very idea of judging drama by some 'lowest-common-denominator':

> [I]f exegesis is valid only if it can be perceived by the least enlightened, much drama criticism, including a vast body of Shakespeare interpretation, would have to be discarded. . . . [T]he text must finally be judged on whatever meaning can validly be found in it by its best readers. (*Four* 226)

And, in a hint that typology is not the only exegetical tool victimized by such arguments, he asserted that "we must be aware that what we discover through erudite scholarship would often have been available in the perceptual set of the most ordinary medieval spectator" (*Four* 226-7).

The more typological criticism moved toward positing a culturally informed Medieval audience familiar with typological significances, the more the traditional definition of typology needed to be re-examined. Richard Emmerson's four-fold critique of what he refers to as "Auerbachian typology" (after Erich Auerbach) has gone far in redefining Medieval typology. All of Emmerson's critiques move away from the idea that typology was an erudite exegesis reserved for the scholars of the day and therefore toward the growing notion that Medieval society was culturally coherent and rich, and that Medieval people partook, to a greater or lesser degree, in that richness.

The first feature of Auerbachian typological interpretation to which Emmerson objects is the notion that typology always links an Old Testament type with a New Testament antitype. Emmerson says that this strict view of typology ignores the richness of typological connections that Medieval people saw between different New Testament figures and even between non-scriptural events and the New Testament ("*Figura*" 9-10). If typology is a cultural component, rather than an esoteric game, then certainly Medieval people would find typological significance in non-Biblical sources. In a Christian sacred system of culture any event might point to Christ and the New Testament, since every moment is informed by God's purposes.

16

The second objectionable feature of traditional typological criticism is that it dismisses literary and mythological symbols that function typologically by insisting on a strict historicity for typology (Emmerson, *"Figura"* 10-11). Though, strictly speaking, type and antitype should both be historical, a similar epistemology of mediation and connection exists in many Medieval literary forms. Indeed, that all things have more meaning to them than is instantly and literally perceivable forms the basic sense of Medieval epistemology. Clifford Davidson writes that when communities put on the Mystery plays "they deliberately were looking beyond the immediate toward the existential realities which they saw as distinct from what could be perceived through immediate sense perception" (*Creation* 192). In other words, the kind of connection that links the type and antitype in typology is not a special epistemological case in Medieval thought.

The third mistaken feature of Auerbachian typology that Emmerson notes is the emphasizing of the type over the antitype. Most typological persons or events have Christ and his ministry as the antitype. Emmerson's reference to Hugh of St. Victor on the subject is apt, explaining that typological ordering does not follow historical ordering, since from a typological perspective Christ is the source and focus of all things (*"Figura"* 12). In a cultural system best described as 'Christian' the natural emphasis of any interpretive method is to reveal the truth of Christ and his earthly mission. This is especially true for late Medieval Christianity which adhered to the notion of a mystical unity of time. In the words of Richard Collier: "[S]ince every moment expresses the eternal, unchanging will of God, every moment is connected analogically with every other moment" (206). The nature of this view of time on which typology rides grew from Christ's own typological statements in the New Testament and is discussed at length by Erich Auerbach, George Poulet , V. A. Kolve and Richard Collier. All of these critics argue that what unifies time is God's eternalness, and what unifies all history is the intervention in history of Christ. In this view of time all historical meaning is derived from the truth of Christ. Emmerson notes:

> The New Testament event remains constant, and it is the search for the Old Testament *figura* that distinguishes typological from tropological and anagogical interpretations. (*"Figura"* 11-12)

The New Testament antitype is Truth to be revealed; the type is just the pointer to that truth. If we are to find a Medieval world view among the common folk, it undoubtedly is a Christian (albeit Medieval) world view, with Christ as the central source of its explanations of things. For typology this means that the antitype must be the focus of typology. The York cycle bears this out in that the plays that run from the Annunciation to the Ascension make up roughly three-quarters of the York text.

The fourth Auerbachian feature that Emmerson critiques is the view that typology is somehow more noble than the other levels of Medieval allegory, and that the other allegorical levels should not pollute the concreteness of typology with their abstractions. Emmerson finds that typology in Medieval literature is always intertwined with tropology and anagoge, as well as other epistemologically similar methods of representation. He argues that Medieval exegesis worked well because its theoretical foundations were universal, while specific interpretations were local and occasional for specific audiences. Emmerson sees Medieval hermeneutics as part of a dynamic system of cultural interpretation through which the Medieval world understood itself, with more emphasis on the interpretive product of exegesis, rather than a strict application of narrow exegetical rules (*"Figura"* 9-16). Strictly speaking, Medieval hermeneutics is the *application* of the four levels of allegorical significance, the literal, the typological, the tropological and the anagogical, to a text, especially the Bible; the four levels of meaning exist as a foundational given in the epistemology of the culture.

The foundation of the many reinterpretations of Medieval literature and culture in the latter part of the 20th century is the insistence that in dealing with Medieval works and theorizing on Medieval audiences, we are dealing with a culture profoundly different from our own. David Bevington, in "Why Teach Medieval Drama?" from the MLA's *Approaches to Teaching Medieval English Drama*, writes of how the view of Medieval drama in his lifetime has changed from the politically charged, pro-protestant, post-romantic view of the plays "as a product of a childish and superstitious Medieval world," a way that does not "challenge the prevailing ideology," to a culturally interpretive methodology:

> Instead, we ask our students to consider a civilization that differs strikingly from their own, and we ask them to consider whether a civilization capable of producing the Gothic cathedral and Geoffrey Chaucer could have lacked its own sense of form and coherence. Was not the drama coherent, too, according to an intuitive set of principles . . . ? (153)

Bevington's cultural attitude toward Medieval drama is representative of the general attitude of the volume. Kathleen Ashley encourages us to see the drama as "cultural performance" in which "a society dramatizes its collective myths, defines itself, and reflects on its practices and values," and says that by the fifteenth century lay appropriations of Christian ritual were widespread with the Christian myth providing the iconic dialect for the whole society (57-8). Using Mary Douglas's definition of cosmology as the root of meaning in society, Ashley finds in the Mystery cycles the perennial self-defining impulse in culture. The context for the drama, claims Ashley, is the entire culture which it reflects and defines: "In essence, the teacher of Medieval drama must become a social historian or an anthropologist" (64). Martin Stevens in the same volume encourages critics of the drama to "rely on a wide spectrum of cultural history" and claims that the drama, as the most composite of art forms, is our best window on Medieval life and thought ("Medieval" 45). Such criticism has opened the door to a complete re-evaluation of the nature of Medieval culture. The old stereotype of culturally ignorant Medieval commoners and isolationist elite scholars with little intercourse between the two has given way to a view of the Middle Ages in which "the distinction between what the elite and the folk knew and did was far less rigid than it became in the early modern period. Popular culture was everyone's culture, especially in festive context" (Ashley 65).

The opposing view, that the poor were culturally ignorant or even 'without culture,' has at its roots a view of the Middle Ages that is warped by the problems of modern socioeconomic divisions and derives from the defunct models of cultural evolution promoted by the Social Darwinists and the elitist humanism of Matthew Arnold. The very word 'medieval' was made fashionable by Victorian historians who would have us believe that 'modern' European culture had somehow escaped the cultural matrix altogether to reside in a transcultural, transhistorical reality. In a movement parallel in some ways to the post-colonial movement in literature, many critics are in the process now of rescuing our Medieval ancestors from the politically charged stereotypes of the past designed to justify present social power structures. To approach Medieval culture as a primitive and therefore inferior version of ourselves is academically foolish and politically reactionary.

An example of this typical cultural disconnect is that critics such as Williams and Manly often point to widespread illiteracy in the Middle Ages to argue against granting "erudite" knowledge to the masses. Yet it is wrong to equate illiteracy in Medieval England to the illiteracy that plagues many underprivileged people in our day. To be illiterate in our hyperliterate society is indeed a great disadvantage since we rely on literacy as the major tool of transferring cultural knowledge, but in other societies cultural knowledge is disseminated in other ways, such as through oral traditions, visual arts, and ritual. Meyers mentions this as part of his response to Williams: "[I]lliteracy does not mean stupidity. Nor are the illiterate necessarily uninformed, especially in a society used to getting its news by hearing rather than reading" (264). Meyers notes that Mirk's *Festial* cites Augustine fifteen times as well as citing Bernard, Gregory, Jerome, Bede, Chrysostom, Anselm and Ambrose (264).

The view of Medieval culture that sees typology as erudite would also have us believe that all culture is imposed from the top of society downward, with the masses gleefully accepting and passing on to their children the cultural tools that scholars give to them (on whatever crude level they can understand). This is the familiar view of Matthew Arnold in which only the *crème de la crème* is actually 'culture' rather than the whole milk bucket. The post-colonial critic Edward Said has refuted Arnold's view of culture, showing that it is inherently combative, pitting the elite few against everyone else in a clash over what the culture will hold true (10-11). Even in our day of electronic media and global cultural empires, the cultural and political elite cannot impose a uniform culture on even the most homogenous of societies. That the basics of Medieval cosmology and epistemology were a conspiracy of the powerful is, to me, unthinkable. That these plays were approved by so many people (the great and the lowly) and played before so many people for so many generations and, in the case of York at least, at such great bother and expense, is the best evidence that they indeed reflected society's view of itself during that period. If we find in the

Medieval mystery plays evidence of typological concerns and other hermeneutic connections, then it is because these interpretive methods were part of how the culture of the time interpreted itself. And, indeed, the late Medieval period was one of great interpretive offerings in art and thinking, filled with many attempts to understand the human experience and its relationship to heaven and to nature. The age experienced great revivals of earlier ideas, especially those found in Augustine and Boethius, with an emphasis on understanding human and divine will, the epistemological significance of the Fall, the experience of community, the understanding of the Bible and a general resurgence of interest in the visual arts, literature, music and science. We may find in the mystery dramas evidence of all of these late Medieval interests and concerns.

The Mystery cycles, then, were not primarily didactic or prescriptive, but primarily performative, evoking the common cosmology of the day, not imposing culture from above. V. A. Kolve writes that though we need the critical help of some understandings that are now esoteric, the cycle drama in its day was neither erudite nor for the learned, nor was it didactic: "The machinery of learning is little evident in these plays, though subtleties of theological understanding are apparent everywhere . . ." (265). Recently Sarah Beckwith has argued that the York plays deny the very possibility of an imposed theology, "of divine authority unrelated to a penitent community;" rather, they are a communal "conversation" with all the inherent "risks of conversation," using "physical procession not just to display a social order but to fight over how it should be made up. . ." (xvii, 3). The discourse space the drama opens is a ritual space where cosmology is defined and therefore created. Mary Douglas insists that even in common discourse, cosmology is always contested as it is presented (*Implicit* 3-4). Such ritual space cannot be opened from above nor imposed. Indeed, a communal struggle to produce meaning is at the core of the nominalist attitude of English culture.

II. The Divine Word of God

This evocative, ritual nature of the York cycle can be easily demonstrated by examining the opening pageants in which the unchanging, eternal God with his divine speaking brings all creation into existence. From a linguistic perspective, the language of these plays is performative rather than merely declarative. Yet a semanticist would also ask if the performative discourse indeed has the illocutionary force of performance. In a strict sense of the word this might not be the case, yet the performative nature of the discourse is effective symbolically and ritualistically within the cultural context of late Medieval York. The character of God might not actually perform the creation in the opening plays, but he does ritually create the cosmology of the culture. Richard Homan insists that the difference between drama and ritual is that the ritual is by itself sufficient to change individuals and society as a result of its production (304-5). So, the performative nature of the discourse does have the illocutionary force of performance on the ritual level, producing and contesting social cosmology.

The dramaturgy of the York cycle is fully tested by the representational demands of the opening scene of the first play—no less than the appearance of God himself and his bringing into creation the heavens and angels. In the first stanza God announces who he is and what his basic attributes are.

> I am gracyus and grete, God withoutyn begynnyng,
> I am maker vnmade, all mighte es in me;
> I am lyfe and way vnto welth-wynnyng,
> I am formaste and fyrste, als I byd sall it be.
>   My blyssyng o ble sall be blendyng,
>   And heldand, from harme to be hydande,
>   My body in blys ay abydande,
>   Vnendande, withoutyn any endyng.
>   (I, 1-8)[2]

The representation of an ineffable being is a somewhat curious and disarming concept, and, indeed, the very notion of representing God on stage in later years caused such social anxieties that it was forbidden by law in England from the suppression of the cycles until the twentieth century. Following that social lead, early critics saw the representations of God in Medieval drama as crude and blasphemous, a typically 'Catholic' idolatry. Collier, in the opening of his discussion on the poetry of the York cycle, complains about Kinghorn's description of God in the first York pageant as "such as one might associate with the Apocryphal Old Testament God if one were an illiterate and untravelled peasant living in feudal Yorkshire six hundred years ago" (Kinghorn qtd. in Collier 21). Collier then uses this same opening material to demonstrate that the York cycle is beautifully poetic when understood within its context. He points out that the speech creates an image of a God who is "decorously motionless" yet whose words are dynamic and filled with "declarative sureness" (21). Collier points to the use of participial forms which "create an equally strong sense of process, of potential" (21). The word choice establishes structures that echo throughout the cycle and create a solid cosmological foundation for more creations to come.

In showing the beauty of the poetry, Collier has demonstrated the ritual nature of the speech. The first thing the character of God creates is himself. This is culturally reflective, not prescriptive or primarily didactic. In the second and third stanzas God as a consequence of his Godly qualities creates the heavens and the angels.

> Sen I am maker vnmade and most es of might,
>   And ay sall be endeles and noghte es but I,
> Vnto my dygnyte dere sall diewly be dyghte
> A place full of plente to my plesying at ply;
>   And therewith als wyll I haue wroght
>   Many dyuers doynges bedene,
>   Whilke warke sall mekely contene,
>   And all sall be made euen of noghte.
>
> But onely þe worthely warke of my wyll
> In my sprete sall enspyre þe mighte of me;
> And in þe fyrste, faythely, my thoughte to fullfyll,
>   Bayneley in my blyssyng I byd at here be
>   A blys al-beledande abowte me,
>   In þe wilke blys I byde at be here
>   Nyen ordres of aungels full clere,
>   In louyng ay-lastande at lowte me.
>
> Here vndernethe me nowe a nexile I neuen,
>   Whilke ile sal be erthe. Now all be at ones
> Erthe haly, and helle, þis hegheste be heuen,
>   And that welth sall welde sall won in þis wones.
>   (I, 9-28)

Here we have language that is clearly performative. The God character is orally creating a visual setting for this first play, but also a cosmological setting for the entire cycle, indeed, the basis of the society's cosmology. All of this rapid development of oral picture and basic cosmology is dependent on the familiarity of the story and the cultural world view into which it fits.

This does not mean, though, that there is no creativity or commentary in the retelling of the basic and familiar. Indeed, the presentation of cosmology always entails interpretation. Collier explores the positive aspects of formulaic language, the clarity and generality that, even though a normative amalgam, give the drama a profoundly creative power (52-3). On a deeper level, Ashley adheres to Victor Turner's belief that ritual is a "subjunctive mood" for culture, that in dramatizing the collective cultural mythology the presenters are "possibly considering alternative ways of behaving and believing" (57). I would take the "possibly" out of the statement and argue that the retelling of mythology *always* entails cultural interpretation and therefore a critique of existing social cosmology.

Certainly if we are going to have a story about God and his acts, one would anticipate it beginning with God's creation of the Heavens and Earth and the beings that dwell in them, but would the audience anticipate his self-creating opening stanza? Why must God say who he is through announcing his name and qualities at the beginning of the play? For the same reason that Shakespeare's Moon in *A Midsummer Night's Dream* must tell us that "this lanthorn doth the horned moon present" (V: 240).[3] And, indeed, a man represents God as a lantern represents the moon. Man is created in God's image, just as a lantern mimics the lights of the sky. The one can represent the other with the appropriate cuing, but their differences are great enough that nothing beyond representation is possible. It would not do for the character of God to appear and with no self-definition begin to command things into being. Whatever costume, mask and iconography the player might be wearing would be insufficient to establish the representation of God, and in this way the drama attests to the creative power of the spoken word in a Biblical context. A lantern can represent the moon because it too gives off light, albeit incomparably less light. A man can represent God because he speaks, as does God, although human speech pales in creative power to God's. God's speaking brings forth all Creation. Human speech is here creating a representation of that creation, yet by creating that representation the character "performs" the defining and interpreting of the social cosmology. This representation of the creative productivity of God's speaking is similar to the creation of the Earth in Genesis, but more closely resonates with the beginning of the Gospel of John:

> In the beginning was the Word, and the Word was with God, and the Word was God. The same was in the beginning with God. All things were made by him; and without him was not anything made that was made. (I: 1-3)

"The Word" that John refers to is both the power of God and the Incarnation of that power in the body and life of Jesus Christ, which John indicates in the fourteenth verse: "And the Word was made flesh, and dwelt among us . . . ." The "Corpus Christi," then, which is the theme of the cycle, is implicitly present from God's first speech of creation. This resonates well with Beckwith's contention that the cycle recalls "the eucharistic imperative" and twists the sacrament of the Body of Christ through the streets of York, transforming the cultural presence of Christ as it invokes that very presence (1).

In this first play, words indeed do what no set or prop could begin to accomplish. Collier notes:

> [G]iven the nature of the action in the Creation play, effects of staging would inevitably be symbolic . . . . Therefore, throughout the play [. . .] it is the poetry, what the audience hears, that carries the action of the play. (26)[4]

Collier finds these qualities in much of the York cycle and argues that

> the restriction on movement on the pageant stage used at York means that the poetry itself frequently has to sustain the theatrical interest and even, when the action is vast in its dimensions and significance, to perform the actions for which it substitutes. (26)

Hence, the drama relies on commonly held images and notions—a poor teacher for the uninitiated, but an effective evocation of the sacred cosmology common to the society.

The second play has the same ritual qualities as the first. Indeed these qualities are even more pronounced in this second play since it consists of a single, long speech by God, most of which is a poetic rendition of the creation of the Earth in Genesis. Again, this play begins by the character of God announcing who he is (this time bilingually):

> *In altissimis habito*,
>   In the heghest heuyn my hame haue I;
> *Eterne mentis et ego*,
>   Withoutyn ende ay-lastandly.
>   (II, 1-4)

He then reviews the fall of the angels, followed by a declaration that he will show forth his power by bringing about the creation of the world simply by bidding it so. Again, the semantic register of the language is performative:

> Syne þat þis world es ordand euyn,
>   Furth well I publysch my power:
> Noght by my strenkyth, but by my steuyn
>   A firmament I byd apere,
> Emange þe waterris, lyght so leuyn,
>   þere cursis lely for to lere,
> And þat same sall be namyd hewuyn,
>   Wyth planitys and with clowdis clere.
>   þe water I will be sent
>   To flowe bothe fare and nere,
>   And þan þe firmament
>   In mydis to set þame sere.
>   (II, 29-40)

The rest of the play goes on in similar fashion with God bidding creation into being through the acts of the fifth day.

All the wonders presented in these first two plays of the cycle may only be represented in a stylized fashion. Nothing could create "the illusion of reality" for such scenes. That they can even be represented with a few icons and a few dozen lines of verse is a product of the familiarity of these things to the audience. The language of the plays is communal and simple, not esoteric. The actions presented were familiar from sermons and the visual arts (among other sources), and the purpose behind the plays was cultural and communal—a society satisfying the desire to publicly display the workings of its cosmology. The cuing, then, of that cosmology, whether through typology, visual iconography or the philosophy and theology inherent in the text, is easily produced because these signals are part of the interrelationship of meanings that make up the culture, not esoteric impositions from clerical sources.

What we truly wish to discern is what the experience of the plays was like for the Medieval playgoer. As Davidson points out in his article "Positional Symbolism and English Medieval Drama," in which he comments on several modern productions of Medieval plays, this is not completely possible:

> Not all of the meaning is capable of being recovered, since the drama's role in religious festival [. . .] will be foreign to modern experience. One writer, reviewing *The Mysteries*, has insisted that "medieval spirituality is not recapturable in the twentieth century." ("Positional" 74)

Nonetheless, just as those who wrote, performed and viewed these plays found, we cannot live without the past, even though we cannot fully recover it. At best we can construct representations of it for ourselves.

Interestingly, this level of meaning, the literal experience of reality that we so desire to recover from the past, would have been, from the Medieval perspective, the least important level of understanding, the literal level being merely that which can be understood by human experience and unaided reason. Earlier stereotypes of Medieval people saw Medieval interest in meanings beyond the physical and literal as evidence of foolishness and a rejection of this "vale of tears." But this is untrue. As Bonaventure points out, each hermeneutic function is present in all the others, and they cannot entirely be separated (Clopper 227). Medieval interest in typological, tropological and anagogical levels of meaning did not negate the literal world; rather, they enhanced the richness of meaning present in all things. From the Medieval perspective all things are riddles filled with hidden wisdom, and all knowledge is brought about by the active mind reaching to find the meaning in things. D. W. Robertson writes:

> [A] work of art was frequently a problem to be solved. . . .
> Lactantius wrote, "it is the business of the poet with some
> gracefulness to change and transfer actual occurrences into other
> representation by oblique transformations," so that he represents a
> "truth veiled with an outward covering and show." This statement
> was frequently repeated during the Middle Ages. . . .
> (*Preface* 15-16)

Though this "husk and kernel" epistemology is most often applied to
fables and fictions, it represents the basic Medieval belief that knowing must be
an active process of discovery. Commenting on the congruity given to all events
by the mystical unity of time, which in the plays gives rise to the creative use of
anachronism as well as typology, Collier notes the active nature of these cuing
systems: "As the plot unfolds, the audience is encouraged to discover analogies
among the discrete scenes and between those scenes and its own present moment"
(193). What unites all the scenes, of course, is what unites all the allegorical
levels of meaning, and is indeed, in Medieval culture, the root and pattern of all
meaning: the nature of God, great and gracious, all knowing, all powerful, creator
of all things, without beginning or ending. The representation of God is the first
image the cycle gives, and it is the root meaning in the culture, the basis from
which the rest of the meaning of things will be built. By performing the creation
of physical cosmology the character of God ritually defines the social cosmology,
creating a communal space for the social production of meaning. In this sense
these plays are ritually performative rather than pedantically didactic. That these
productions of meaning were flawed, contested, even at times self-sabotaging,
supports rather than refutes the claim that they held great cultural resonance for
their audiences.

Chapter 2
Typology and Boethian Time in the Structure of the York Cycle

In "Typology and English Literature" Richard Emmerson has satisfactorily demonstrated that typology does not stand apart from the other levels of Medieval allegory. Emmerson examines the *Biblia Pauperum* and the *Speculum Humanae Salvationis* as typical popular works of the late Middle Ages and concludes that "[f]igural interpretation is almost always accompanied by tropological interpretations [. . .] and occasionally by anagogical promises" ("Figura" 24). This is in response to those whom Emmerson calls the "Auerbachian" critics who exalted typology over the other levels of allegory, considering it of special importance in interpreting Medieval works to such an extent that they generally disparaged and ignored tropology and anagoge.

Though Emmerson is correct in pointing out that all the levels of allegory were used together and that the critic should not ignore the others, there is evidence that typology was heavily favored by Medieval artists and poets, and that, indeed, typology holds a special importance for the Medieval world view. Emmerson's own statement (above) indicates that typology is present in the works he studied more often than the "almost always" tropological accompaniment or the occasional anagoge. He also mentions that the tropological moralizations in the *Biblia Pauperum* "are brief although ever present" ("Figura" 24). Since in this chapter I propose to examine how typology informs the structure of the York cycle, we should examine more carefully the arguments that posit typology as the key and distinguishing element of Medieval allegory and cosmology. Since the York cycle evokes cosmology, the importance of typology to the cycle's structure should parallel the importance of typology in the cosmology of the culture.

I. The Importance of Typology to Medieval Cosmology

In the article "Figura" Erich Auerbach shows that though the word *figura* was used in various ways in the ancient world, its great significance to Western cosmology arose when Tertullian and other church fathers began to use it in the sense that it was used in Medieval typology as "something real and historical which announces something else that is also real and historical" (29). This usage developed from the early Christian historicists' arguments against spiritualism in order "to show that the persons and events of the Old Testament were prefigurations of the New Testament and its history of salvation" (30). Auerbach says that Tertullian was

> hostile to spiritualism and refused to consider the Old Testament as mere allegory; according to him, it had real, literal meaning throughout [. . .] and the figure had just as much historical reality as what is prophesied. (30)

This was opposed to the views of Origen and others who believed that the Old Testament should not be taken literally but read in the abstract, allegorical fashion commonly used to interpret Homer and Hesiod.

Tertullian, of course, did not invent figural interpretation, which is hinted at in the Gospels and propounded by Paul in his Epistles, but the victory of typology over abstraction among the early patristics gave Christianity a persuasive explanation of human history, one which rescued historicity and spirituality from the cyclical fatalism of the classical philosophies. Herbert Muller in *Freedom in the Ancient World* asserts:

> For the Gentiles in particular, Christ gave new meaning to history. He was a Person, not an impersonal Necessity. Unlike the gods of all the other mystery religions, he was clearly a historic founder. Unlike them he did not die annually, cyclically; he might appear to do so in the ritual Mass, or later in Passion plays, but Christians always knew that his crucifixion was a unique historic event. . . . [N]one of them adopted the view of history as endless cycle: a view that might offer the solace of resignation to the uniform, inevitable fate, as Marcus Aurelius insisted, but that was more likely to make history seem meaningless, pointless, as the

> melancholy of Marcus testified. After the sack of Rome by Alaric,
> St. Augustine emphasized the futility of the cyclical theory,
> arguing that only Christianity made history meaningful. (322-3)

Auerbach similarly argues that if those who interpreted the Old Testament abstractly had won out, Christianity "would necessarily have lost its conception of a providential history, its intrinsic concreteness, and with these no doubt some of its immense persuasive power" (52). The older allegorical methods were stale, having been done for Homer and Hesiod *ad nauseam*; only typology "was assuredly a fresh beginning and rebirth of man's creative powers" (56). At the same time it had the advantage of being rooted in ancient texts and centuries of history (58). These qualities gave typology the power to transform the cosmology of the late classical world with positive connotations for the development of Western culture: "Consequently the attitude embodied in the figural interpretation became one of the essential elements of the Christian picture of reality, history, and the concrete world in general" (Auerbach 53).

Much of the success of typology and history in Medieval Western Europe undoubtedly came from the adoption of these attitudes by Augustine who, Auerbach says, "favored a living, figural interpretation, for his thinking was far too concrete and historical to content itself with pure abstract allegory" (37). Muller argues that what helped Christianity gain converts and rise in power during the falling of the classical world lies partly in the hope offered by typological history:

> No doubt [Christians] were buoyed up primarily by their hope of
> personal immortality [. . .] but they were also buoyed up as no
> pagan could be by the belief that the coming of Christ was the
> climax of history, the key to the whole meaning and purpose of
> man's history on earth. (321-2)

The abstract levels of allegory had been used in Greek exegesis for centuries when typology began to be pushed by Tertullian and others. It is this "new" hermeneutic, then, that colors all the others, making it a uniquely Christian outlook and placing Christ's intervention in history at the heart of Medieval Western European cosmology. Emmerson is right that "pure typology" is a misunderstanding (and in all fairness, he is not so hard on Auerbach as on the

Auerbachians), but Muller and Auerbach are right to see the special place of typology in Medieval culture, and this is why there is so much typology in Medieval art and literature, and why the study of typology has been such a rich vein for critics to tap. The revival of Augustinian and Boethian thought in the 14th century made typology especially attractive in the age that gave rise to the Corpus Christi cycles. Commenting on the importance of typological ordering to Corpus Christi drama Martin Stevens concludes:

> Typology is not only a key to the meaning of the Corpus Christi cycles; it is the essential dramatic structuring device upon which the native English dramatic tradition is built. (*Four* 233)

Typology, then, is potentially the most useful key to understanding the unique cosmological perspective of the Middle Ages, and, therefore, it should be an important tool for interpreting the York cycle. Yet, there are a few critics who, though they accept typology as a legitimate tool for the Medieval critic, do not believe that it is especially suited for interpreting this work. Stevens, for one, holds up the N-Town cycle as the "Corpus Christi cycle in which typology is brought to its full power as a dramatic structuring device" (*Four* 257), and does not even mention typology in his analysis of York. More generally, D. W. Robertson argues that what we see as typology in Mystery drama is actually "tropological verisimilitude," whereby one understands morality as imitating Christ ("Question" 225). Collier argues that "the York dramatists are primarily concerned with the process of events rather than their patterns," and that God's ordaining of time and history "is shown through the motif of prophecy and fulfillment rather than that of figures and their fulfillments" (208).

All of these observations are legitimate; yet, they do not indicate that typology is absent from the York cycle, but rather suggest that typology is not particularly emphasized in the plays. However, traditional typological motifs from the Old and New Testaments are used throughout the cycle. Though Kolve's discussion of the principles of selection for Old Testament stories in Corpus Christi drama has received many legitimate and important critiques, the widespread use of these few episodes in Medieval arts of all kinds indicates some cultural sense is operating. Clifford Davidson's work with contemporary glass

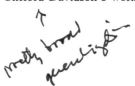
pretty broad generalist

and its relationship to the drama has strengthened the contention that typology informs all episodic art of the Middle Ages. If Robertson's "tropological verisimilitude" and Collins's "prophecy and fulfillment" are present in these instances, then they also must depend on a typological foundation, or at least have typological resonance that would have been available to audiences. Perhaps the York dramatists did intend to emphasize prophecy in their rendition of sacred history; nonetheless, the episodes available to them for appropriation were greatly defined by artistic traditions that grew from typological interpretations of history.

Certainly, other cycles, such as N-Town and Wakefield, overtly showcase typological significances in a way that the York cycle does not. However, this very contrast highlights the ubiquitous and ambient nature of typology in the cosmology of Medieval culture. Meyers discusses God's typological explanations in the Wakefield Annunciation play as an example of the direct use of typology in Mystery drama, but then notes that what is directly announced in Wakefield, is implied in York:

> [T]hese are only explicit discussions of the type, not the implicit presumption of the knowledge of typology that we can draw from, say, the York cycle, where the play of the Annunciation begins with a prologue telling of prophecies of the Messiah, rehearsing salvation history from the fall to the time of John the Baptist, where every indication is given that a new age of the world is beginning. (267)

The York cycle is the most conventional of the four extant cycles. That typological orderings are implicit in the structure of York is a testimony to the wide-spread understanding of typology among Medieval people and to the importance of typology in Medieval cosmology. Ruth Nissé in her analysis of the surprising similarities between the Lollards and the York playwrights argues quite convincingly that the York plays do not represent orthodoxy (427-8). Similarly, Sarah Beckwith argues that the York plays deny the very possibility of an imposed theology, "of divine authority unrelated to a penitent community;" rather, they are a communal "conversation" with all the inherent "risks of conversation," using "physical procession not just to display a social order but to fight over how it should be made up . . ." (xvii, 3). But should an argument against orthodoxy preclude the presence of allegorical exegesis in the plays? Only if we assume that such constructs are purely orthodox and solely exegetical. If we find typology operative in the structure of the cycle, then we must conclude it is not an orthodox imposition but rather a construct of the social cosmology so ubiquitous and ambient that it is not part of the contested social space of the cycle, though the meanings it constructs might well be contested.

Typology can be seen in the York cycle through several of its structural elements, especially the Boethian Time - Eternity contrasts in the cycle's frame and the discrete but recursive nature of the episodes. These interconnected elements arise from Medieval beliefs about the nature of the Eternal God and his relationship to the temporal world. What unites all the episodes of history in the temporal world is God's purpose. What this demands of a system of historical representation is that its elements be episodic, discrete, additive and recursive, with each element containing a microcosmic reflection of the macrocosmic whole.

II. Discrete, Recursive, Microcosmic Episodes

Typological criticism of any art usually deals with the specifics of how Old Testament types prefigure New Testament antitypes. In the plastic arts this entails the direct juxtaposing of icons of a type and its antitype. Patrick Collins argues that dramatic prefigurings cannot be considered typological since their fulfillments are not immediately present ("Typology" 298). Even so, there is an implied typology in the drama inherent in the cultural context of its performance. Typology is a tool of representation that demonstrates the cosmological ordering of time and space in Medieval culture. Auerbach says that "*the attitude embodied in the figural interpretation*" is an essential element of Medieval cosmology (53, emphasis added). Typology is a manifestation of an Augustinian, Christian interpretation of history, a tool of representation and interpretation that arises from the cosmology. It is this "attitude embodied in the figural interpretation" that I am looking for in the York plays, not necessarily episodes of juxtaposed types and antitypes. It is this "attitude," this ordering of history, that informs the structure of the cycle.

Corpus Christi drama is an episodic art form, comprised of a series of discrete artistic events, much the same as cathedral glass, murals, picture books and processionals, and the drama probably inherits this from its processional roots. Critics have shown that some Corpus Christi cycles were not processions on wagons, and in the case of N-Town, Alan H. Nelson argues that its structure and mode of performance "are a determined effort [. . .] to move away from the episodic style which is their inheritance from the predramatic procession of pageants" ("Configurations" 147). However, if N-Town represents a resistance to the episodic nature of the genre, York, on the contrary, literally revels in it. Though there are still many questions about the logistics of York's presentation, the general consensus remains that the York cycle was presented on pageant wagons and at various posts along a processional route. Indeed, for the York cycle, the processional quality is as inextricably connected with its ritually festive context as its episodic nature is connected with the cosmological context that the ritual reinforces.

Medieval episodic art often has been misunderstood because its structure is strikingly different from the cause-and-effect structure of modern drama and narrative. Auerbach in "Figura" discusses how typology reveals a "vertical structure" in which mortal effects are a result of eternal causes:

> [T]he individual earthly event is not regarded as a definitive self-sufficient reality, nor as a link in a chain of development in which single events or combinations of events perpetually give rise to new events, but viewed primarily in immediate vertical connection with a divine order which encompasses it . . . . (72)

Following Auerbach's lead, V. A. Kolve revealed the basic structure of the Corpus Christi drama in his seminal work, *The Play Called Corpus Christi* (1966):

> The events chosen for dramatization are those in which God intervenes in human history; significant time, it follows, becomes simply the point of intersection between these actions, the will of God expressed in time from outside time, by which a connection deeper than temporal causality is stated. (119)

Richard Collier in *Poetry and Drama in the York Corpus Christi Play* demonstrated that this linear but non-causal sense of time informs York:

> It is [. . .] the medieval Christian understanding of time which sees time as an artifact of God through which He, in whom there is no distinction of times, makes Himself known to man. As the manifestation of the eternal will of God, events are not self-sufficient moments in a linear process. . . . [T]hey are part of a process moving forward in time . . . . But earthly events are most importantly recognized as being connected "vertically" with God and His eternal order which encompasses and informs them all. (205-6)

However, this type of cosmological and literary structure is foreign enough to modern readers that its implications are often missed. Daniel Poteet complains that cosmological explanations for the elements and structure of Medieval drama are often overlooked, that many of the qualities in Corpus Christi drama that are condemned, such as the absence of sequenced causality and plot development, "are in fact iconographic in their tendency to objectify a particular medieval attitude toward time and timelessness . . ." (247).

It is important to understand that the episodic, discrete structure of the drama is meaningful, not arbitrary nor the result of an amateurish lack of structural sense. Stevens notes that the discrete episodes and the movement between them replicate the *sedes* and *platea* structure of liturgical drama (Four 68-9). Clifford Davidson demonstrates the drama's affinity with other episodic visual arts, in particular stained glass, in his foundational work *Drama and Art; An Introduction to the Use of Evidence from the Visual Arts for the Study of Early Drama*. Like the cathedrals, Corpus Christi drama is a representation of God and a rendering of his relationship with humanity, an anagoge that must, then, necessarily make use of the other levels of allegory, especially typology, to achieve the anagogical effect.

The discrete nature of the episodes also fits well into the nominalist epistemology of the late Middle Ages in which knowledge must be actively discovered from oblique representation. Stevens's observations on the epistemology of typology are apt:

> Transferred to the popular religious cycles, [typology] encourages the playwright to envisage one scene or character in terms of another, and it invites the reader/spectator to discover the "matches." The result is a whole new dramatic form in which scenes, characters, and even plots are linked implicitly as a fundamental structuring plan. The playwright counts on this structure to hold together the disparate parts of his play and to encourage the spectators or readers to make the connection for themselves—to see, for example, that Lucifer, Pharaoh, Caesar, Herod, and Pilate are basically the same person, and thereby to bind together the evil of the fallen angel with that of fallen man and to provide a nexus for the cycle in which the basic conflict between Satan and God is renewed again and again until it is finally resolved. (*Four* 232)

Hidden within each figure is a statement of the problem of the Fall and the solution of Christ's Atonement. The discrete episodes reveal an implicit structure in the whole of the cycle, an all day riddle about the human predicament, the answer to which is "Corpus Christi."

A typological structure, then, can admit any number of figures; it is additive and expansive, drawing its strength from variant repetitions of similar elements. Though Kolve discovered a theoretical proto-cycle, a basic form that all extant Corpus Christi cycles (and the records of a few lost cycles) contain, all extant cycles add to this core group. This is not to say that there are no indispensable episodes or that they are freely interchangeable, but within the prescription some additions and subtractions can take place because each element is recursive and microcosmic in relation to the whole. Stevens compares this structure to the poignantly repetitive nature of Shakespeare's *Henriad*: "Here, as in the mystery cycle, the additive style allows us to build a macrocosm out of matched microcosmic events" resulting in "a true *theatrum mundi*" (*Four* 233). Stevens notes that the York cycle makes the City of York into a microcosm of the world since it converts the streets of York into "the *platea* of a *theatrum mundi*" (*Four* 69).

The first York play establishes the basic pattern for all the rest. In it God declares who he is and creates joyful places and beings, but some beings rebel against him and are separated from the others into a place of misery. This is the first Creation, Fall, and Dividing. The second play begins with a recapitulation of the first: God announces who he is, declares that he has created many realms and beings, and that some fell because of pride and had to be separated from Heaven (I, 1-16). The second stanza describes the awful state of the fallen angels and the happy state of those that dwell with God. God declares of the fallen that "þare mys may neuer be amende/ Sen þai asent me to forsake" (II, 17-18), echoing the same explanation in Play I (132-3). This division of Heaven and Hell that came from the first Fall sets up important similarities and contrasts with the human Fall soon to be played. In the third stanza, in response to the Fall of the bad angels, God initiates a second Creation, that of the Earth and life in it. This is a complete microcosm declaring God's supreme creative power: God creates, evil destroys, God responds by healing with more creation. This establishes the basic mnemonic recognized throughout the cycle.

Play III begins by God recapitulating the first five days of creation from the previous play. He then says that the world is imperfect, lacking "a skylfull best" to join with him in loving the world. To remedy this deficiency he creates Adam and Eve out of earth, and telling them that they have "lordschipe in earthe," places them in paradise. The fourth play consists of God's commandments to Adam and Eve, promising bliss for obedience and sorrow and death for disobedience, echoing the same promises to the angels in Play I. Play V completes the cosmology with the second Fall, that of Adam and Eve. It begins with Satan declaring his intention to counter God's new creation with new sin and destruction. Eve's recounting of God's commandments reviews the previous play's events, and Satan's appearance heralds a repetition of his fall.

If any play sequence represents immediate cause and effect then it is the movement from Play V, The Fall, to Play VI, The Expulsion. Nonetheless, the effects are not simply a matter of course—they are God's first judgment of humankind, and therefore define the essentials of human ontology, physically, morally and epistemologically. The moral dichotomy of this fallen state echoes the Heaven and Hell dichotomy created by Lucifer's fall, but with one essential difference: People are forgivable; their fallen state is potentially amendable. Beginning with the next play, Cain and Abel, each Old Testament play contains the same struggle between good and evil, the same human capacity for obedience and disobedience, and the resulting blessings and curses for the two human groups which echo the blessings and curses of the obedient and disobedient angels.

These first seven plays take us from the division of Heaven and Hell after the fall of the Angels to the division of humanity in the actions of Cain and Abel after the fall of their parents. The plays contain the essential ingredients for the Eternity / Mortality cosmology and the doctrine of sin and salvation. In production these plays would have been entirely discrete with different sets, casts and a fair amount of logistical chaos in between; yet they adhere by forming the essential ingredients of Christian cosmology. The repetition of icons, figures, phrases and similar actions become a mnemonic for the thematic presentation. Each play is a piece of the argument, but also a reflection of the whole, having a hermeneutic consistency reflecting normative cultural cosmology. In the words of Richard Collier:

> Everything the audience sees taking place is willed by God. Everything that is willed by God is seen to take place. In simple terms, these are the controlling aspects of the plot of the plays . . . . . (215)

The rest of the Old Testament plays repeat the theme of fall and destruction with God extending salvation to the faithful, which both echoes the action of the opening plays and anticipates the coming of spiritual salvation through Christ. These plays (VIII-XI) dramatize the stories of Noah and the Flood, Abraham and Isaac, and Moses and Pharaoh, and have been written about extensively in terms of their figural significance.[5] In the two Noah plays we find another sequence of destruction and salvation. Noah and his wife are the new Adam and Eve commissioned to recreate the world. Collier writes:

> What God has in mind as He prepares to send the flood is a recapitulation of His first Creation: "wirke þis werke I will al newe" (VIII, 24). Through Noah's obedience, he and his family come to participate in this re-Creation as Adam and Eve had participated in the first. At the end of the play of the Flood, Noah's sons ask how they are to live since they are the only ones left alive on earth. . . . Noah, as *imitator Dei*, gives the same instructions to his family that God had given to Adam and Eve. (204)

In Abraham and Isaac we find the clearest prefiguring of God's offering of his Son as a surrogate for human sin. Collier calls the Abraham and Isaac play "[t]he most extensive reflection of typology in the York plays" (208), and, indeed, the typology of this episode has been written about more than any other, most notably the relationship between the surrogate sheep found caught in a briar and Christ as the Lamb of God. Collier notes that this symbolism is repeated and reversed in the play of the Purification of Mary when Joseph suggests that Jesus will replace the sacrificial lamb required by Mosaic Law (210-11).

The Moses and Pharaoh play again prefigures salvation, and is later echoed by the leading of the saved out of Hell in the Harrowing of Hell play, linking the captivity in Egypt with the captivity of sin and death. Moses's confrontation of words with Pharaoh is repeated in Christ's verbal overpowering of Hell in the Harrowing episode. Rosemary Woolf writes:

> Pharaoh's connection with Satan in the Harrowing of Hell is displayed, not merely by the extraordinary frequency with which he swears by the devil, but also by a small nexus of vocabulary which is conspicuously used in both plays . . . . Pharaoh's dismissal of the claims of Moses [. . .] have precisely the jeering tone that Satan was later to use in rejecting the idea that Christ would release the souls from hell; and the calm asseverations of power with which Christ then responded are similarly anticipated in the speeches of Moses to Pharaoh. (154)

After Moses comes The Annunciation and Visitation. The beginning of this play (XII) is a long speech by *Doctour* which reviews the action of the earlier plays, adding a few more prefigurings and prophecies from the Old Testament in preparation for the fulfillment of all figures in the coming of Christ to the Earth. Davidson suggests that this might have served as the introduction to a truncated rendition of the cycle, sans Old Testament plays (*Creation* 64-5). However, though the Doctor's introduction may have served this purpose at some time, its repetitiveness need not be explained in this way since it fits the additive, recursive structure found throughout the cycle.

Play XIII, Joseph's Trouble about Mary, repeats one more time the human fallen condition on the eve of the coming of the Fall's remedy. Joseph and Mary are another Adam and Eve, Joseph representing the 'old man' of the flesh, lost and powerless as a result of Adam's Fall, and Mary, the obedient maidservant of God correcting Eve's original disobedience. Collier notes that the image of the married couple is echoed in Adam and Eve, Noah and Uxor, and Mary and Joseph, and that they represent the dissolution and then reintegration of harmony in the world (202-3).

Plays XIV through XLII (the bulk of the cycle) dramatize the fulfillment of figures in the life and ministry of Jesus. This is the essence of typology. The earlier plays are a prefiguring set up for the cycle's focus, the intervention of Eternity into mortality through the Corpus Christi, Eternity incarnate in the Body of Christ. After play XLII, The Ascension, comes Pentecost which demonstrates how the once obscure figures have become clear in the light of Christ's mission. Play XLIV through XLVI concern the Death, Assumption and Coronation of the Virgin, which demonstrate the actual salvation of humanity. They emphasize the enigmatic quality of the new Age of Mercy, for in the play of her death Mary, representing humanity, is still subject to the pains and sorrows of mortality. In the following plays she is brought into the glories of Heaven. Her Celestial Coronation signals the Cycle's re-entry into Eternity and the fulfillment of God's promises to the righteous. Though life in the fallen earthly state continues, the inheritance lost by Adam and Eve has been regained by Mary and Christ. The Virgin's abiding in glory in Heaven echoes the glorified state granted to the obedient angels of the first play.

The final play (XLVII) is The Last Judgment. It is also entirely recursive, beginning with a recapitulation of the whole Cycle; however, this recapitulation is not a part of the episodic structure of human history, but rather a part of the Eternal frame within which the episodic structure rests. That the powerful Mercers guild owned this play attests to its importance to the cycle. As the final judgment from Eternity of all history, this play establishes the framework from which the action of the whole cycle is defined. A detailed examination of the play will reveal the Eternal frame which surrounds and defines the episodes of history.

III. The Representation of the Eternal Frame in the York Mercer's Play

In the Introduction to their modernized edition of the York Cycle, Richard Beadle and Pamela King mention that some critics see this last play as unnecessary because "Christ's work of redemption has been completed [. . .] and the Cycle's spiritual messages fully stated" (267). Beadle and King do see at least one purpose: to remind the audience that "the time of mercy [. . .] is not of infinite duration" (267). Others have hinted that it serves to unify the Cycle, giving it what Collier calls "a sense of resolution and fulfillment" (241). In light of the typological structure of the cycle outlined above it becomes obvious that the unity this last play provides is the Eternal frame, the vertical context for all the discrete, mortal episodes. This setting is a Boethian Eternity where God sees all history as one sight. The play achieves this representation by flattening character, space, and action into unambiguous dichotomies. We have returned to Eternity from where the cycle began and have an extra-historical frame of reference for the history presented. This frame reveals the world view implicit in the vertical structure, the cosmology that is represented by typology.

In the first eight stanzas, God reviews history and includes all the essential components of the doctrine of good and evil, sin and repentance, damnation and salvation. God's historical and theological review of the world establishes the context by which a judgment by God of what has gone on in history is both just and necessary. By recapitulating history in his speech, God is also demonstrating his perspective, according to the Boethian model found in *De Consolatione Philosophiae* Book V prose 6 in which God sees all history at once, Eternity being a state apart from time, rather than forever time:

> Aeternitas igitur est interminablis vitae tota simul et perfecta possessio, quod ex collatione temporalium clarius liquet. Nam quicquid vivit in tempore, id praesens a praeteritis in futura procedit nihilque est in tempore constitutum, quod totum vitae suae spatium pariter possit amplecti, sed crastinum quidem nondum apprehendit, hesternum vero iam perdidit; in hodierna quoque vita non amplius vivitis quam in illo mobili transitorioque momeneto. . . . Quod igitur interminabilis vitae plenitudinem totam pariter comprehendit ac possidet, cui neque futuri quicquam absit nec praeteriti fluxerit, id aeternum esse iure perhibetur idque

necesse est et sui compos praesens sibi semper assistere et infinitatem mobilis temporis habere praesentem.
(Buchner, ed. 109, ll. 13-20, 27-33)

[Eternity is the simultaneous and complete possession of infinite life. This will appear more clearly if we compare it with temporal things. All that lives under the conditions of time moves through the present from the past to the future; there is nothing set in time which can at one moment grasp the whole space of its lifetime. It cannot yet comprehend tomorrow; yesterday it has already lost. And in this life of to-day your life is no more than a changing, passing moment. . . . What we should rightly call eternity is that which grasps and possesses wholly and simultaneously the fullness of unending life, which lacks naught of the future, and has lost naught of the fleeting past; and such an existence must be ever present in itself to control and aid itself, and also must keep present with itself the infinity of changing. (Cooper, trans. 115-6)]

In the first stanza God identifies himself as the creator of the world and all it contains in a mnemonic echo of the opening plays of the cycle. He says that when he first made human beings they were good, since they were made in his image (XLVII, 1-8). The primitive state is goodness, since God, the origin of everything, is supremely good. He then explains how it is possible for people to become evil: "I gaffe hym wittes hymselue to wisse . . ." (XLVII, 10). Because people have free will and knowledge, they may freely choose good or evil.

In stanza three God recounts the Fall of Man and how evil came into the world. Man was "begilid thurgh glotony" to eat the apple (XLVII, 21-2). The sin of pride is implied by the line, "He wende haue bene a god þerby/ He wende haue wittyne of all-kynne thyng/ In worlde to haue bene als wise as I" (XLVII, 18-20). Man is gluttonous for knowledge and power, and prideful in believing he can obtain all knowledge. This is the dilemma of human ontology and epistemology: having "wittes," the ability to know, but no certain knowledge. This is why humankind can be "begilid" and fall into sin.

Throughout God's review of history he refers to human beings only by the generic "man." Adam and Eve are not mentioned, nor any individual. God mentions only the main character of history, Christ, whom he calls simply "my sone" (XLVII, 27). Satan as well is conspicuously absent from this review: Judgment Day is for humanity; Satan and his crew are already damned and do not have grace available to them. In the first play, when Satan and his followers have fallen, God says: "For sum ar fallen into fylthe þat euermore sall fade þam,/ And neuer sall haue grace for to gyrth þam" (I, 132-3). The absence of mention of the Devil also indicates that human beings cannot blame devils for their actions, and the Bad Souls blame only themselves for their sins: "Oure wikkid werkis þei will vs wreye . . . / Oure dedis beis oure dampnacioune" (XLVII, 129, 138).

The Fall brought sin and damnation into the world which made necessary Christ's mission to bring repentance and salvation, the theme with which most of the Cycle is concerned and which is recounted in stanzas four and five of the play. If the cycle is framed by Eternity, then Christ's mission represents the road back to Eternity, what Jerome Taylor calls "the wonders by which the divine King reintegrates the creaturely kingdom disobedient to his law. . ." ("Dramatic" 156). After Adam and Eve are exiled from paradise and become subject to death, the scene of the plays is the world, not Eternity, until The Coronation of the Virgin, immediately preceding the Doomsday play.[6]

In stanza six God recounts Christ's Atonement which ushered in the Age of Mercy: "Sethen haue þei founde me full of mercye,/ Full of grace and forgiffenesse . . ." (XLVII, 41-2). But in stanza seven God sees that the world is full of vanity; people do not give thought to the fact that they will die (XLVII, 49-52). In stanza eight he says that there are no more people in the world who are willing to take advantage of the New Law by repenting:

> And vnethis fynde I ferre or nere
> A man þat will his misse amende.
> In erthe I see butte synnes seere,
> Therefore myne aungellis will I sende
> To blawe þer bemys, þat all may here
> The tyme is comen I will make end.
> (XLVII, 59-64)

The age of mercy has ended, because the inhabitants of the world no longer ask for mercy.

This opening recapitulation of history from a generic, theological perspective outlines the basic tenets of Christian doctrine and presents the context for judgment. It also shows God as seeing all history at once from Eternity. This

Boethian ordering of Eternity and Time is significant to this play because it is the basis for Boethius's argument for free will and human accountability. A vertical structure to history could suggest that human beings have no free will without the Boethian argument for free will based on God's residing entirely outside of time. God ends his speech in stanzas nine and ten by sending his angels to gather all the world, "And sounderes þame before my sight . . ." (XLVII, 73). They are to be divided left and right, the evil and the good, to receive judgment, "To ilke a man as he hath serued me" (XLVII, 80). This last line of God's speech foreshadows the criteria by which the Son will judge, the dichotomy of Matthew 25.

In stanzas eleven and twelve two angels announce Doomsday to the world and command all creatures to come forth: "Body and sawle with you ye bring,/ And comes before þe high justise" (XLVII, 91-2). This is the physical resurrection coming to all, both good and evil as is indicated in John 5:29: "they that have done good, unto the resurrection of life; and they that have done evil, unto the resurrection of damnation." Humankind coming forth to judgment is represented by the generic characters *I* and *II Anima Bona*, and *I* and *II Anima Mala*, who enter and speak in stanzas 13-22. *I Anima Bona* speaks of the resurrection joyfully: "Body and sawle togedir, clene,/ To come before þe high justice" (XLVII, 99-100). On the other hand *I Anima Mala* regrets their existence: "Allas, allas, þat we were borne . . ." (XLVII, 113), and sees in the resurrection the source of eternal pain: "Nowe mon neuere saule ne body dye,/ But with wikkid peynes euermore be betyne" (XLVII, 135-6). The *Animae* are not shades, but physical, resurrected beings, subject to pains and joys, echoing the detailed pains and joys of the good and bad angels described in Plays I and II. And like the first dividing of good and evil, this division is permanent. It is only within time and history that human faults are amendable; Eternity is entirely dichotomized.

Though the physical nature of resurrection allows audience identification with the *Animae*, the facelessness of these characters is significant. Divided, the *Animae* become symbolic elements in the emblem the play creates. They are faceless because in Eternity all the historical hierarchies and labels are effaced. All of the diverse characters of the Cycle have been flattened into two types. The *Animae* do not say who they were in the world, nor do they refer to specific acts that got them damned or saved, but describe themselves and their deeds

46

genericaly. We may assume that during their speeches the good and bad souls intermingle because *II Angelus* begins stanza twenty-three by ordering them to divide: "Standis noght togedir, parte you in two!" (XLVII, 169). Time has stopped; the multitude of characters present in the earlier plays has been reduced to the dichotomy of good and bad souls; space is now dichotomized, with the bad on the left and the good on the right. The pageant wagon is becoming an emblem created by symbolic characters and a symmetrical division of the physical setting. The emblem is completed when through the hanging clouds the crucified Christ descends over the center of the wagon on a swing.[7] God explains that he is taking the form of the crucified Christ to judge the world because it is the symbol of his atonement: "þis body will I bere with me—/ Howe it was dight, mannes mys to mende,/ All mankynde þere schall it see" (XLVII, 182-4). The emblem receives its final embellishment when Jesus calls upon two Apostles to witness the judgment, and devils appear, eager to collect the "full grete partie" of sinners (stanzas 27-30).

In stanzas 31-36 Christ presents the five wounds suffered for the world's misdeeds, and rehearses his scourging and crucifixion. Christ continually reminds the other players, and the audience, that he suffered these things for them, to atone for their sins: "þus was I dight for thy folye--/ Man, loke, thy liffe was to me full leffe" (XLVII, 267-8). Then he reverses roles with his audience, asking: "All þis I suffered for þi sake--/ Say, man, what suffered þou for me?" (XLVII, 275-6). The Christ character has offered the iconographic elements that identify him as the Savior, and, in rehearsing the sacrifice made out of love for man, establishes both the authority to judge and the criteria for judgment. Stanzas 37-48 contain the central action of the Mercers' Play, the Judgment. Christ judges mankind in the manner presented in the Twenty-fifth Chapter of Matthew. The good souls are invited into paradise because they performed the Corporal Acts of Mercy for Christ when he was in need; the bad souls are damned because they did not show mercy to him. When both groups ask to know when they have done or not done these things, Christ answers that what they have done to their fellow human beings, they have done to him.

In all four extant Mystery cycles the Doomsday play ignores the dramatic scenes of the end of the world described in the Apocalypse in favor of the simple dichotomy in Matthew 25, and Davidson notes that this "was fairly typical of the ways in which the Doom was most commonly pictured in the visual arts" (*Creation* 182). This iconography gives the play an impact which comes from a carefully controlled symmetry, creating a textual and visual emblem of the Judgment. The play also achieves an identification with Deity based on the criteria of judgment: whether or not one's response to human suffering emulates the Deity. The effect on the audience is personal, rather than sensational. All of the action of the Cycle is reduced to whether one has served or neglected others, whether one has demonstrated the charity which Christ represents.

In this representation of judgment the mystery of salvation is revealed in its simplicity. The audience leaves the feast of Corpus Christi reminded of specific, commonplace things that they may do to achieve salvation, the Corporal Acts of Mercy. This also reminds them of the identification that Deity makes with them. Christ is every person who reaches out for help, and every person who helps, both one who pleads for mercy, and one who grants mercy. Identification with God is inextricably linked to identification with the community and a reaffirmation of their inescapable interdependence. The community indeed becomes a microcosm of the universe and each member a microcosm of the struggle between good and evil.

The forty-ninth stanza closes the play and the entire cycle with God (in the form of Christ) announcing: "Nowe is fulfillid all my forþoght,/ For endid is all erthely thyng" (XLVII, 373-4). This resonates with the opening play in which God begins creating in order to "fullfyll" his "thoughte" (I, 19). He then leads the way to heaven while the bad souls are driven into the Hellmouth. The action of the cycle begins in Eternity, is exiled into the particulars of History, and then returns to its origin in Eternity. Eternity is God's perspective. The human perspective is necessarily flawed and limited; God's perspective is necessarily the complete Truth. This anagogical representation is achieved emblematically by flattening character, space, and action in the Mercers' Play into strict divisions of good and evil, a dichotomizing of the dramatic elements representing an exit from mortal Time and entry into the framework of Eternity. It is only from this Eternal frame that the discrete episodes of the cycle reveal their connection in a vertical structure. The recursive recapitulations and typological prefigurings of the episodes, then, constitute intentional microcosmic reflections of God's timeless perspective. It is this Boethian cosmology that fosters typology. This "attitude

48

embodied in figural interpretation" is implied throughout the Cycle by its discrete and recursive episodes and their setting in the framework of Eternity.

This cosmological ordering embodied in typology certainly marks a significant division between the world as constructed by the late Medieval citizens of York and the social cosmologies of the readers and interpreters of these texts in our day, and though we cannot fully or truly recover the past, we nonetheless are driven to attempt it as part of our construction of who we are and what we might become. Such frames of reference, limited or even flawed as they may be, are relevant to our lives. Interestingly, the limitations of human epistemology enacted in Medieval drama resonate well with post-modern struggles to both perceive and recognize the limits of perception. Hence, though typological analysis in no way circumscribes a "Medieval world view" nor precludes the presence of competing contemporary discourse, it undoubtedly allows us, in de Grazia's terms, to put "a frame around a temporal span" and "see something [of relevance] inside it" (8-9).

Chapter 3
Fifteenth-century Mystical Nominalism in the York Cycle

As representations of cultural beliefs of the age, the great mystery cycles of the late Medieval period in England describe the human condition through displaying the Biblical accounts of humanity's fall from grace in Eden and subsequent salvation from the Fall through Christ's atonement. There is a nominalist epistemology implied in the Fall and Redemption argument of the York cycle. The cycle, as a whole, presents the argument that human free will and the divine purposes of heaven co-exist from a perspective in which human action, though indeed free, is entirely meaningless except when it conforms to God's purposes. This attitude toward cosmology and epistemology follows Ockham's critical nominalism, the prevailing philosophy of late Medieval Western Europe, a philosophy that developed as a critical response to the extreme realism of the 13th century. This shift in philosophical attitude permeated the culture of 15th century Western Europe, including the mysticism of Nicholas of Cusa and the art of the Flemish painters. Ultimately the argument over whether these plays are a clerical product or truly folk literature is moot. Clerics were not isolated scholars inhabiting a world far removed from the common people, nor did common people reside in some simplistic, a-cultural existence devoid of understanding. Finding nominalist attitudes in these plays does not indicate that they were clerical products. Insisting that they were produced by common folk does not preclude any analysis that would connect the social cosmology inherent within them with the scholastic thought of they day. Was there a single author for much of the passion plays in the middle of the cycle, an author that many have called the "York Realist"? Though many plays in this part of the cycle share a strikingly similar style, the existence of such a person will probably never be adequately demonstrated. Yet, it hardly matters when one addresses the question of the prevailing world view of the people who produced these plays over nearly three centuries. Many of the plays not assigned to the supposed "York Realist" nevertheless reveal a social cosmology rife with typological structure, as shown in earlier chapters, and equally imbued with an epistemological attitude best described as nominalist.

That some recent critics wish to use New Historicism to clip any connections between scholasticism and folk art shows a failure to understand the often counterintuitive conclusions of the localizing anthropology of theorists such as Clifford Geertz and Mary Douglas. Insisting that folk art does not or cannot resonate with scholastic productions would seem to echo modern social cosmology in highly competitive Low Grid / Low Group cultures such as our own, cultures in which the insistence on inherent equality inevitably becomes a smoke screen for the contradictory view that there exist natural superiors and inferiors, a division marked by hidden insulation that truly compartmentalizes society and drives many in academia to fashion themselves as a people apart. Medieval societies, on the contrary, were High Grid / High Group cosmologies where insulation was transparent. Enshrined caste systems rather than promoting cosmological division in society, promote coherence in social cosmology since the obvious divisions are a social given, not a product of competitive desire.[8] As late as the 1990s most critics were struck by the relative coherence of Medieval culture and society, despite local variation, when compared with modern times. The recent abandonment of this idea would seem to be a product of the increasingly competitive and therefore esoteric nature of modern academia as we push ever further down grid. The intense irony of this situation would be amusing if it were not so damaging to the health of academia and a healthy view of the past. In contrast, the nominalist epistemology of late Medieval culture insisted on the communal production of meaning and therefore pushed communal unity in social cosmology against any thought of dividing the world between the educated and the common. The pervasive cycle dramas themselves are the ultimate expression of this communal, nominalist, unifying epistemology.

I. The Medieval Epistemology of the Fallen Mind in the York Cycle

Medieval tropology concerns epistemology, the nature of human knowledge. As typology reveals the meaning of human history through the direct intervention in history of the Son, tropology represents the revelation of truth in the life of the individual through the direct intervention into the human life of the Holy Spirit; these together lead one to the anagogical knowledge of the ineffable Father. Bonaventure revealed the connection between the epistemological divisions of allegory and the ontological division of the tripartite God in *De Reductione Artium ad Theologiam*. Sr. Emma Therese Healy's commentary offers a telling description of the *"lumen superius"*:[9]

> The meaning of sacred text is not always limited to the literal interpretation, for the language of the Bible, *under the inspiration of the Holy Ghost*, is used to express many truths beyond the power and scope of human reason. In addition to the literal sense, many passages contain an allegorical, a tropological, and an anagogical meaning. . . . Hence all Sacred Scripture teaches these three truths: namely, the eternal generation and Incarnation of the Son of God, the pattern of human life, and the union of the soul with God. (100-1, emphasis added)

Tropology extends the epistemology of the Medieval explanation of world history to the microcosmic history of the individual life. Just as the truth of history is revealed through Christ's intervention, without which it is incomprehensible, it is through the Holy Spirit's intervention in the life of the individual that the truth of one's life is revealed, without which life remains incomprehensible.

Typology may be emphasized in Medieval art because it is the sense that differentiates the Medieval allegory from the classical, but in terms of the functioning of the culture, Emmerson is to some extent correct in saying that all allegorical levels are equally important. The typological truth of Christ's mission escapes the human mind without the continually renewed intervention into individual lives of the Holy Spirit testifying of Christ. Yet the two are inseparable, because tropological revelation of moral and ultimate truth becomes possible only through Christ's typological intervention. The purpose of both is to reconnect the literal existence of humanity with God:

> Faith teaches that one purpose of the Incarnation of the Son of God was to restore to man, at least essentially, his primary relation to God. The first man by his faculties of memory, understanding, and will, participated in a finite manner in the divine immortality, intelligence, and free will. In addition to this natural likeness, he

> possessed supernatural gifts, chief among which was sanctifying grace whereby the Holy Ghost dwelt in his soul. The indwelling of the Holy Ghost brought with it many other gifts, such as the theological virtues of faith, hope, and charity, the seven gifts of the Holy Ghost and *freedom from ignorance*, sorrow and concupiscence. Original sin not only despoiled the soul of the likeness to God which conferred grace but it also weakened the natural faculties which reflected the image of God, for which reasons there was need of a spiritual re-creation before fallen man could attain his destined end. (Healy 101, emphasis added)

The theology of salvation relies on a human ontology best described as a "fallen state." One of the chief characteristics of the Medieval attitude toward the story of the Fall is an emphasis on the epistemological condition of fallen humanity rather than the ontology of moral corruption. Within the York cycle the mortal state is morally ambiguous; human characters commit evil deeds more often out of ignorance and human weakness than a malicious desire for evil. Reacting against Rossiter's description of the "fiendish" crucifiers in York (XXXV, 135-42), Stanley Kahrl writes:

> I [. . .] find no evidence of fiendish delight in this language, for [. . . w]hat these men are involved in is not Christ's pain, but getting on with the job. . . . The only emotion expressed is the satisfaction that the man they have been given to fasten to a cross is fastened down to stay. (96)

V. A. Kolve sees a similar pattern for all of mystery drama:

> At certain times, natural man is categorically at enmity with the divine; at other times (and they are more dangerous to theological order), he simply holds the divine to be categorically irrelevant to him. (217)

The fallen state may at times include maliciousness, but it is principally a state of ignorance, having the ability to know, but no certainty of knowledge. This description of human ontology and epistemology is inherent in the idea of the Fall, that human beings are epistemologically less able now than they once were, or can potentially become. Collier writes:

> Once there was a time, the English clerk Dan Jon Gaytryge
> explains toward the end of the fourteenth century, when men like
> the Angels had known God directly. But now, he continues, "all þe
> knaweyng þat we hafe in þis werlde of Hym, es of herynge and of
> lerynge and of techyng of oþer." (Collier 62)

V. A. Kolve also discusses this epistemological effect of the Fall in the
Introduction to *The Play Called Corpus Christi*:[10]

> God had made man a rational creature that he might "know" Him
> and share in that way the bliss of heaven. Before the Fall, such
> knowing had been immediate and without obstruction; with the
> Fall, that perfection of knowledge, that intimacy and likeness was
> lost. (3)

This kind of thinking elevates epistemology to such a level that it threatens to
absorb metaphysics: to "know" God is to possess God, to achieve a union with
Truth without which all human knowing is merely probable at best, and mostly
spurious. Augustine, by emphasizing personal biography, psychology, and the
primacy of the 'will,' moved Western thinking toward an experientialism and a
critical examination of human perception. The shift in early modern times from
seeing the description of humanity contained in the Fall as an epistemological
description to emphasizing the moral corruption caused by the Fall leads many to
misread the Medieval period's emphasis on humanity's fallen state as also
metaphysical. Uncertainty, blindness, a mistrust of the world—these are all part
of the traditional negative stereotype of the Middle Ages, but from the perspective
of post-modern thinking, which is also profoundly aware of the limited, discrete
and relative nature of perception, we may begin to reanalyze Medieval
perceptions, especially the late Medieval nominalism which emphasized
epistemology over metaphysics.

Balancing the negative description of humanity as fallen is the salvation
introduced by Christ's atonement, and, again, there is an epistemological flavor to
the 'light' of salvation that shines in the 'darkness' of the world. Augustine's
teachings about the divine illumination of the intellect have also been mistaken in
modern times for a purely metaphysical description of a purely mystical

phenomenon, though most scholars reject this attitude in favor of a more epistemological reading:

> It is [. . .] universally recognized that the 'divine illumination' is not in essence, and on all levels of cognition, either supernatural or mystical . . . . Augustine is peremptory on the point; the divine illumination, at least on its lowest levels, is the way of knowledge for all men. (Knowles 41)

These two opposing descriptions of humanity, then, are the essential ingredients of the Medieval view of the human epistemological condition: that humanity is in a fallen and blind state, but that human beings are capable of divine understanding through God's intervention. This description of fallen yet saved humanity is prominent in all the English Mystery cycles, especially in York. Davidson writes that the most prominent feature of the plays between the Fall and the Annunciation is "the marked alteration in the human condition following the fall from the idyllic state experienced in the Garden of Eden" (*Creation* 39-40). This alteration begins with the play of The Expulsion (VI).

In this play Adam and Eve lament the loss of Eden. In a long speech Adam lists their losses and then despairing, says "On lyve methynkith I lyffe to lange,/ Allas þe whille" (103-4). In this dark state Adam suddenly becomes aware of the epistemological impact of the Fall, being separated from the sure source of truth:

> A, lord, I thynke what thynge is þis
> That me is ordayned for my mysse;
> Gyffe I wirke wronge, who shulde me wys
>   Be any waye?
> How beste will be, so have Y blisse,
>   I shall assaye.
>
> Allas, for bale, what may þis bee?
> In worlde vnwisely wrought have wee,
> This erthe it trembelys for this tree
>   And dyns ilke dele!
> Alle þis worlde in wrothe with mee,
>   Þis wote I wele.
>   (VI, 105-16)

All that he can "assaye" from the world over which he once ruled is that it is entirely wroth with him. Deprived of understanding, and separated from the counsels of Heaven, Adam honestly asks: "If I work wrongly, who shall guide me in any way?" The entire foundation of his existence has given way, and he falls into bickering with Eve for the remainder of the play. They have no other counsel except each other and cannot agree on anything. They are, it would seem, epistemologically completely lost, knowing nothing but uncertainty and fear. Davidson writes that this play "focuses most upon the moral and physical disaster brought upon mankind" (*Creation* 41). I would say, however, that what Adam demonstrates in this play is better described as an epistemological disaster: he cannot be certain of the morality of his choices and cannot get from the Earth his physical needs because he no longer has the understanding that came from his communion with God in Eden.

In the Old Testament plays that follow characters either obey God (whether they understand or not) and are drawn to him, or they eschew God's counsel and become more removed from him. This is the division established by the Cain and Abel play. Nonetheless, the good characters are in the same fallen state of epistemological blindness as the bad characters, and many people choose wrongly not out of evil but out of mortal frailties.

Noah's wife refuses to enter the ark because she thinks it is all foolishness and she would rather go to town (IX, 81), needs to gather her utensils (109-10), and wants her friends and relatives to come with her if she must go (141-44). Davidson writes that this "farce is calculated to set off the absurdity which marks the behavior of those who, self-deceived, fail to understand the desperation inherent in the fallen condition of man" (*Creation* 52). Uxor's disgruntled chattering about petty concerns and the physical struggle between Noah and his wife represent the continual movement, directionless and restless, of fallen human beings, always in need, always unsatisfied, their minds alternating among a myriad of petty concerns and enterprises. This "'rennyng' energy," writes Kolve, "is an important part of the drama's conception of human nature after the Fall" (213).

In the Moses and Pharaoh play Moses reacts to God's commands with polite human excuses:

> A, lord, syth, with thy leue,
>   þat lynage loves me noght,
> Gladly they walde me greve
> And I slyke boodword brought.
>
> Therefore lord, late sum othir fraste
>   þat hase more forse for þam to feere.
>   (XI, 129-34)

God tells him not to be afraid to announce his commandments to Pharaoh and promises to protect him, but still Moses replies that the plan will not work: "We, lord, þai wil noght to me trayste/ For al the othes þat I may swere" (139-40). Moses is willing to obey but in his fallen way doubts that obedience will be efficacious.

Perhaps the best representation of fallen humanity in the York cycle is the character of Joseph in the play of The Nativity. When the Holy Couple arrive at the stable, Joseph is distraught about the run-down and drafty condition of their dwelling. He decides to go out into the night to find light and fuel for their need. Joseph prays for God to guide him and then sees the Light of Christ coming from the stable:

> A, lord God, what light is þis
>   þat comes shynyng þus sodenly?
> I can not saie als haue I blisse.
> When I come home vnto Marie
>
>   Þan sall I spirre.
> A, here be God, for nowe come I.
>   (XIV, 78-83)

J. W. Robinson writes:

> Now, while he is out looking for earthly light, it ironically happens
> that the Light of the World is born. In the midst of his shivering
> and stumbling search in the Place for light [. . .] a great light shines,
> and Joseph returns to Mary to find out what it is. (*Studies* 68)

Robinson notes that this action corresponds with St. Bridget's account in which Joseph's candle gives no light, "the divine light totally annihilating the material light of the candle" (Bridget qtd. in Robinson, *Studies* 68). The epistemological overtones to the light symbolism are pronounced in this play. Joseph cannot adequately provide for his family. He cannot dispel the gloom and cold, nor change their destitute circumstances—what little "human" light he can produce is almost meaningless.

The Flight to Egypt has a similar theme of fallen epistemology. The Holy Family has been commanded to flee to Egypt to protect baby Jesus from Herod; yet in typical human fashion they have no idea which road to take. They express an immobilizing epistemological desperation that echoes Adam's desperation in The Expulsion.

> *Maria*
> Allas Joseph, for greuance grete,
> Whan shall my sorowe slake,
> For I wote noght whedir to fare?
> *Joseph*
> To Egipte—talde I þe lang are.
> *Maria*
> Whare standith itt?
> Fayne wolde I witt.
> *Joseph*
> What wate I?
> I wote not where it stande.
> *Maria*
> Joseph, I aske mersy,
> Helpe me oute of þis lande.
> (XVIII, 173-82)

Joseph then asks Mary to give him the child. He takes the baby in his arms and confidently sets off. He reassures Mary that they will be all right: "Nowe schall no hatyll do vs harme,/ I have oure helpe here in myn arme" (223-4). The symbolic message is clearly displayed in this short dramatic tableaux: human beings are lost in this world, but can find their way by faith in Christ.

The blindness of humanity and the efficacy of Christ's enlightening power are again displayed at the end of his life. The soldiers who crucify Christ are blind to the import of their deed. The best example of this is the blind Longeus,

who in the York account is given a spear and commanded to stab Jesus. Collier
writes:

> Longeus' blindness is imaged in his silent cooperation with Pilate,
> but as he pierces Christ's side his blindness is cured and Pilate's
> blindness is exposed . . . . In the figure of Longeus the play
> presents the most compact and compelling enactment of its
> controlling action as through Christ's mercy he is brought to "se
> þer þe soth in his sight." (184)

The light that cures Longeus's blindness reflects from him to others who by this
miracle see the light of Christ's divinity in the world's darkest moment:

> Like Longeus before him, the Centurion here bears joyful witness
> to the truth of the Crucifixion, which he comes to see,
> paradoxically and miraculously, only in the darkness which he
> describes descending upon the scene. (Collier 185)

In a similar sense Mary Magdalene represents this movement from
obscured human understanding to enlightened revelation in the play of Christ's
Appearance to Mary Magdalene (XXXIX). She seeks Christ but does not
recognize him when she talks to him, mistaking him for the gardener. Only after
he calls her by name and shows her his wounded flesh does she recognize him
and realize the truth of the Resurrection. Christ's atoning sacrifice has brought
salvation from sin into the world, but humanity's understanding has not yet been
healed. Unaided reason still cannot perceive Christ without his direct
interventions and demonstrations.

Throughout Christ's ministry and after the Resurrection, even the Apostles
cannot perceive divine truth with unaided human reason. The York cycle follows
the Bible in that the Apostles, though they believe in Christ and testify of him, do
not truly understand his mission until the Holy Spirit descends on them on the day
of Pentecost. One example of the Apostles' pre-Pentecost blindness is the
confusion of Peter, James, and John in the Transfiguration play. The play begins
with Jesus reminding the three Apostles of the interchange between himself and
Peter (found in Matthew 16:13-19) in which Peter testifies of Christ through the
inspiration of God:

> Þou aunswered, Petir, for thy prowe,
>   And saide þat I was Crist, God sonne,
> Bot of thyselffe þat had noght þowe,
>   My fadir hadde þat grace begonne.
> Þerfore bese bolde and biddis now
>   To tyme ye haue my fadir fonne.
>   (XXIII, 37-42)

Though through his faith and God's grace Peter knew the truth of Christ, he cannot perceive Celestial truth on his own. Before the transfiguring begins Peter says to his companions:

> Full glad and blithe awe vs to be,
>   And thanke oure maistir mekill of mayne
> Þat sais we schall þe sightis see,
>   The whiche non othir schall see certayne.
>   (XXIII, 49-52)

But his next speech, which is after the first speeches of Elias and Moses, indicates that they have not seen anything "certayne":

> Brethir, whateuere yone brightnes be?
>   Swilk burdis beforne was neuere sene.
> It marres my myght, I may not see,
>   So selcouth thyng was neuere sene.
>   (XXIII, 85-88)

Throughout the play the three Apostles dimly perceive what is happening. Afterward Jesus asks them what they saw, and they admit to having understood very little:

> *Petrus*
> We saugh here pleynly persones thre
>   And nowe is oure lorde lefte allone.
> Þis meruayle movis my mynde
>   And makis my flessh affrayed.
>   *Jacobus*
> Þis brightnes made me blynde.
>   I bode neuere swilke a brayde.
>   (XXIII, 187-92)

John says that he knows for certain that two bodies stood by Jesus and said they were from his father. Then, says Peter, a cloud came out of the sky and lighted up everything, and he does not know what happened next. James (Jacobus) says the light stunned them. John argues that it was rather a hideous noise that vexed them. Jesus tells them not to fear and explains that his Father sent two witnesses, "A quyck man and a dede," to testify that he is the Father's Son (194-216). They are Apostles, but still unenlightened, fallen, human beings, and can only perceive within their mortal limitations.

Two examples that show that the Apostles are unable to perceive truth by unaided reason even after the Resurrection are the plays of The Supper at Emmaus and The Incredulity of Thomas. In The Supper at Emmaus (XL) the two pilgrims discuss the events of the Crucifixion in Christ's presence but cannot understand what has happened and do not recognize him. Jesus chides them for not recognizing the fulfilling of the prophecies of Moses, but they still do not understand that the answer to their questions, the physical proof in the resurrected person of Christ, is right before them until after he has left them. This pattern anticipates his words to the Apostles in the Ascension play when he promises them the Holy Spirit but says, "And butte I wende comes noght to yowe/ þe comforteoure of comforteles . . ." (XLII, 165-6). Thomas cannot perceive the truth of the Resurrection until he experiences physical contact with the living Christ for himself. At the close of The Incredulity of Thomas, Christ says that those who believe without seeing will be more blessed, and tells them that he will send them out to preach to the world to convince those that have not seen (XLI, 187-98). However, this will not be possible until the descent of the Holy Spirit at the day of Pentecost.

The most important play concerning the enlightening of fallen humanity is one of the least written about plays in the York cycle, the Pentecost play. This play reveals the human condition by juxtaposing the two states of human mortality: fallen and blind, and saved and inspired. It is in this play that the human blindness we have seen throughout the cycle is finally cured. At the beginning of the Pentecost play the Apostles are in doubt and in hiding, waiting for the Holy Ghost to descend on them. The distress from their uncertainty about what to preach is compounded by their inability to move from their hiding place for fear of their enemies, and later in the play we find that there are some people seeking to kill them. The Fourth and Fifth Apostles explain how they are helpless to defend themselves until the Holy Ghost is sent:

> *IV Apostolus*
> He highte vs fro harme for to hyde
> And holde in hele both hede and hende,
> Whanne we take þat he talde þat tyde,
> Fro all oure foois it schall vs fende.
> But þus in bayle behoues vs bide
> To tyme þat sande till vs be sende;
> Þe Jewis besettis vs in ilke a side
> Þat we may nowdir walke nor wende.
> *V Apostolus*
> We dare noȝt walke for drede
> Or comforte come vs till,
> Itt is moste for oure spede
> Here to be stokyn still.
> (XLIII, 49-60)

They are "stock still," frozen in an immobilizing lack of understanding and power that has been the mark of fallen humanity from Adam's first desperate realization of his ignorance and weakness in the play of The Expulsion to this very moment of restless suspense. Mary responds to their restlessness with comfort, assuring them that her son will help them:

> *Maria*
> He will ȝou wisse to wirke full wele,
> For þe tente day is þis to telle
> Sen he saide we schull fauoure fele
> Leuys wele þat lange schall it not dwell,
> And therefore dred you neuere a dele,
> But prayes with harte and hende
> Þat we his help may haue
> Þanne schall it sone be sende,
> Þa sande þat schall vs saue.
> (XLIII, 64-72)

The next scene shows their physical fears to be real. It is a dialogue between two Doctors who swear by "Mahound" that they will kill the Apostles when they come out of the house.

At this point the Holy Ghost descends on those present as is indicated by the stage direction, "*Angelus tunc cantare 'Veni creator spiritus.'*" Mary breaks out into praise and worship of Jesus, announcing the coming of the Holy Spirit, "Mirthis and trewthe to taste/ And all misse to amende" (107-8). Peter and the other Apostles then express the truth and power that they are tasting for the first time:

> *Petrus*
> All mys to mende nowe haue we myght,
> þis is þe mirthe oure maistir of mente.
> I myght noȝt loke, so was it light--
> A, loued be þat lorde þat itt vs lente.
> Now hase he holden þat he vs highte,
> His holy goste here haue we hente;
> Like to þe sonne itt semed in sight,
> And sodenly þanne was itt sente.
> (XLIII, 109-16)

The other Apostles respond with similar testimonies of new-found power and wisdom. For example:

> *III Apostolus*
> We haue force for to fighte in felde
> And fauour of all folke in feere,
> With wisdome in þis worlde to welde
> Be knowing of all clergye clere.
> (XLIII, 121-4)

The Apostles' newly found power and wisdom is shown through their confrontations with the two doctors who are neither able to condemn them verbally nor attack them physically. At the end of the play the Apostles confidently take leave to the various parts of the world to which they are called. With God's light restored to the human mind, human beings are no longer trapped by ignorance and weakness and can act with wisdom and confidence. This is not a moral salvation, which had already been accomplished by Christ's sacrifice, but an epistemological salvation, the active restitution of humanity's communion with God before the Fall. The human epistemological condition has now been fully defined: fallen into darkness and uncertainty by the loss of Eden, but having the potential for an enlightened understanding of eternal truth through the personal, tropological intervention of the Holy Ghost in the life of the individual. This emphasis on a mystical epistemology resonates greatly with the philosophical milieu of the late Middle Ages.

II. The Nominalist Context of the York Cycle

Though they have their beginnings in the previous century, and were played well into the next, the fifteenth century is the age of the great Mystery cycles in England. The one dramatist who many believe wrote most of the York passion sequence, sometimes identified as the York Realist, was writing sometime early in the fifteenth century.[11] By this time the critical nominalism of William of Ockham and others, arising in England in the early fourteenth century, had spread throughout the Universities of Europe (Knowles 330). A philosophical movement as widespread and deep-reaching as critical nominalism must have reflected the culture of the time, and in turn have become a part of the greater culture's self-defining discourse. Knowles writes:

> [Ockham's] name and his works became famous because they exactly suited the temper of and the tendencies of his age. It was his achievement to do boldly and see clearly what others were attempting or only dimly discerning. (327)

The studies of Erwin Panofsky linking the philosophical shift from Thomist realism to nominalism with the development of Gothic architecture out of the Romanesque are further evidence that these cosmological discourses that seem esoteric today were indeed widely resonant and productive in their context. Panofsky argues that there existed in the late Middle Ages an extended community of literates from various walks of life and social classes who had extensive social intercourse and shared a common discourse dialect, since no branch of human knowledge had developed specialized terms, making the "whole range of human knowledge" available to "non-specialized intellects" (*Gothic* 22-

64

*Good luck
at York!*

3). Panofsky adds that "the entire social system was rapidly changing toward an urban professionalism," providing a meeting ground where priest and layman, poet and lawyer, scholar and artisan "could get together on terms of near equality" (*Gothic* 24). It is exactly this kind of urbanism that grew up in York in the late Medieval period, and with it grew the York Mystery cycle as the major focus of communal life. It is not surprising, then, that within the cycle we find the same cosmology that Ockham, the Early Gothic architects, and the Flemish painters expressed so well in their respective media of communication.

Ockham's epistemology eschews metaphysics, denying the existence of universals and discussing all knowledge in terms of probabilities only (Panofsky, *Gothic* 12-13). This epistemological subjectivism throws the individual back upon the resources of sensory and psychological experience. The ring of Augustinianism in the epistemology of critical nominalism is not surprising as the Augustinian revival that would last well into the modern era was already in full swing. Panofsky writes that in the fourteenth century "[p]re-scholastic Augustinianism (asserting, among other things, the independence of the will from the intellect) was vigorously revived in opposition to Thomas," whose anti-Augustinian tenets were condemned three years after his death (*Gothic* 9).

The common thread between Augustinianism and the critical nominalism of Ockham is an emphasis on the primacy and complete freedom of the will which encourages an epistemology that interrogates the limitations of human perception and the iconographic, mediating nature of all representation. This psychological and process oriented epistemology ultimately resides only in the experience of the individual. It recognizes the extreme isolation of individual experience but also that the semiotic systems which give meaning to experience are communal.

Yet both Ockham and Augustine remedy the loss of metaphysical certainty in two ways, by divine illumination (certain but frighteningly personal) and by the communal production of meaning, an idea that some (perhaps over-ambitiously) credit to Augustine himself:

> Christopher Dawson, one of [Augustine's] many contemporary
> admirers, asserts that he "first made possible the ideal of a social
> order resting upon the free personality and a common effort
> towards moral ends." (Muller 350)

Ockham's epistemology derives its name, nominalism, from the assertion that words do not have a correspondence with any postulated universal forms, but rather reflect a community's production and acceptance of meaning. Knowles notes that nominalism's essential differentiation of "words" versus "things" has its source "in the well known Boethian dichotomy" (11). Renewed interest in Boethius, whose cosmology nicely compliments Augustine's thinking, is even more pronounced in the late Middle Ages than the Augustinian revival itself— indeed, the revivals of both are intimately intertwined in late Medieval thought. Gaytryge's epistemology from a late fourteenth century sermon (quoted above) has an unmistakable ring of the communal production of meaning in its description of the fallen state: "[A]ll þe knaweyng þat we hafe in þis werlde of Hym, es of herynge and of lerynge and of techyng of oþer" (Gaytryge qtd. in Collier 62).

A careful analysis of the York Cycle reveals the ubiquitous nominalist flavor of late Medieval culture. Yet there is much confusion in the scholarship over the meaning and import of critical nominalism, especially how it conflicts with the use of the term 'realism' to describe certain naturalistic elements in the drama. Part of this confusion stems from traditional views, inherited from the Neoscholastics, that misread Ockham's critical nominalism as equivalent to either the nihilistic metaphysics of the earlier Roscellinus or the radical agnosticisms espoused by other late Medieval scholars and mystics who get tossed under the rubric of nominalism.[12]

The American philosopher Charles Sanders Peirce recognized the importance of Ockham's critical nominalism many years ago. However, though his ideas had a large impact on American thinking through William James and John Dewey, the longtime obscurity of much of Peirce's writings has helped delay the re-evaluation of the true impact of Ockham's nominalism on late Medieval thought and the development of the modern world. Much of the temperament of Peirce's pragmatism and semiotics, as well as the philosophies of James and Dewey, drew from the primarily epistemological and experiential philosophies of England. As part of a lecture series on the history of logic delivered in 1869, Peirce discourses on the nominalist nature of English thought:

> The most striking characteristic of British thinkers is their nominalistic tendency. This has always been and is now very marked .... William Ockham or Oakum, an Englishman, is beyond question the greatest nominalist that ever lived ....
> (310-11)

Peirce extols Ockham and Duns Scotus as, respectively, the greatest nominalist and realist logicians who ever lived, emphasizing a common bond of speculative logic in their otherwise opposing views. Peirce finds a similar brand of empiricism in the scientific and mathematical inquiries of Roger Bacon, Francis Bacon, Boole, De Morgan, and the philosophies of Whewell, Mill and Herschel (311). Peirce concludes: "You perceive therefore how intimately modern and medieval thought are connected in England—more so than in Germany or France ..." (311).

English culture, it would seem, did not need a Maurice De Wulf to rediscover the temperament of Medieval scholarship, though the English temperament is nominalist rather than Thomist. Indeed, many who misunderstand critical nominalism are influenced by the love of De Wulf and other Neoscholastics for the Aristotleanism of the twelfth and thirteenth century scholastics and their accompanying jaundiced view of late Medieval thought, what De Wulf terms "the sterility of the period in question" (145). From Peirce's perspective, the *productivity* of late Medieval thinking continues to this day.

Modern movements in cultural semiotics have recently revived interest in the work of Peirce and the many sources that influenced him. There is a direct connection between the rebellion of nominalism against Thomas's orderly realism and the rebellion in our day of semiotic, cultural analysis, informed by pragmatism and anthropology, against the idealist, reductionist formalisms that have informed much modern thinking. This throws an interesting light on the cultural sensitivity and productivity of the York cycle. In a context in which the prevailing thinking does not offer comfortable assurances of epistemological certainty, the communal attempt in the York cycle to define social and cultural typologies in a cooperative display of the basic elements of cultural cosmology is, perhaps, the supreme demonstration of the humanism inherent in the uncertainty of nominalist epistemology. Since no one authority can safely interpret all facets of canon scripture and human experience, truth cannot be imposed by authority, sacerdotal or political, but must continually manifest itself through ritual acts of communal struggle to produce acceptable displays of belief.

Ockham's radical break with the earlier scholasticism was a rejection of all *auctoritas* in favor of direct, personal experience and observation (Panofksy, *Gothic* 69). Peirce in 1869 equated nominalism's break with *auctoritas* with the struggle in his own day between the followers of Herbert Spencer, who believed science must be grounded in an authoritative tradition, and the proponents of the new scientific method, such as Darwin, who developed their theories from systematic, virgin observation (314). To be thrust from the precise and balanced lattices of formalized thought to the socially charged and relative taxonomy of cultural typologies (in the modern sense of the word 'typology') is, perhaps, uncomfortable, but this course, it would seem, is inevitable.[13] Yet, the artistic and literary productivity of the late Middle Ages demonstrates the great potential of nominalist epistemologies to create broad cultural solutions when freed from the strictures of formalist realisms.

The key to the relativist perspective is, in our day as in Ockham's, an emphasis on the interrogation of epistemology that leaves metaphysics to be filled-in by the local cosmology. This perspective also frees modern critics to both examine localized culture and productively speculate on generalizations, the one supporting rather than negating the legitimacy of the other. What formalists fear about relativism is that it threatens to reduce existence to meaninglessness and words to the *flatus vocis* of Roscellinus's metaphysical nihilism.[14] However if one ignores the categorizing tendency of metaphysics for the creative tendencies of an open-ended, self-critical epistemology, words, then, become the opposite of *flatus vocis*, having infinite possibilities of meaning, rather than no meaning at all. For the critical nominalists, as for the modern pragmatists, it is not Roscellinus's void of meaninglessness in which we are lost, but rather we are lost in the infinite possibilities of meaning open to the human mind. Understanding is a matter of constructing truth among the clutter of potential meanings rather than discovering the universal essence of a meaning. It is from this perspective that the "realistic" details present in the York cycle represent critical nominalism. These seemingly spurious details demonstrate the co-existence of Divine will and human agency from a perspective in which human action is indeed free, but entirely meaningless in the divine scheme of things except when it conforms to God's ultimate purposes.

III. "The York Nominalist"

Using the name the 'York realist' to distinguish one supposed author of most of the York Passion sequence (and several other plays) was first proposed by Charles Gayley in 1903, the same writer who coined the name the 'Wakefield Master.' In 1963, J. W. Robinson capitalized the 'r' in 'realist' launching a forty-year debate over what is meant by 'Realist' in this name. The various interpretations of 'Realist' offered by other critics led Robinson to later reconsider the terminology he coined and eventually concede that the dramatist's religious considerations subsume the realistic details (*Studies* 19). In his original article of 1963 Robinson said that it is the personal motivation for character behavior in the plays that identifies this playwright with realism ("Art" 234-6), but in his later work he decided that it was rather the playwright's "unmetaphoring" of the Old Testament prophecies of Isaiah and others, not the seemingly arbitrary detail, that identifies the author as the 'Realist' (*Studies* 31). This later explanation is not very detailed, but obviously deals with an entirely different issue from the gratuitous details in the plays or the 'natural' behavior of characters. This late explanation increases the confusion that the original article spawned rather than resolving any issues, but it was published posthumously and perhaps is not completely developed.

Lately, some critics have doubted whether one person actually wrote all the plays traditionally attributed to this supposed playwright. Much of this doubt, however, arises not from a renewed analysis of the plays themselves; rather it stems from the debate over whether non-clerical writers were responsible for the cycle rather than the supposed clerics. As I have noted in the beginning of the chapter, I believe the debate over whether the writers were clerics or not is somewhat moot. To see clerics as radically different in life and thought from commoners is a mistaken notion long put aside but recently revived for reasons which, I believe, have much to do with present battles over theory and little to do with textual and material evidence from the period in question. In either case, to decide that the writers were not clerics and that, therefore, the plays cannot include allegorical elements or a world view parallel with the philosophical schools of the time supposes that Medieval society was as compartmentalized as ours. Again, localizing analysis and thickening cultural description cannot be allowed to preclude the humanist's or social scientist's program of making sense of the larger scene without undermining the very program that these analytical methods were developed to promote. I assert that even if all the plays in the cycle had different authors, even if they were all commoners, all clerics, or a mixture of both, we should still find within them a cosmology that reflects both the local character of the time and place and resonates with broader definitions of culture recognizable as coherent in their differences from our own local and broad cultural structures. It may be that the commonalities that many see in these plays reside not in a common author but in a common view, coherent within itself but different enough from our own that the lack of consubstantiality gives rise to a growing notion of the structure and boundaries of a social cosmology we recognize as late Medieval Western culture. Localizing culture, after all, is a relative idea that may be focused as narrowly as a household and a season or broad as an empire and an age. All cultural interpretation must reside in differences of culture seen and defined through another culture. The debate over whether or not there was one writer for most of the passion sequence ultimately must stand or fall on stylistic analysis of the plays themselves, though, in a sense, the question may never be answered conclusively unless some presently unknown (and unlikely) material evidence emerges that clearly identifies this supposed author's existence. However, if such an author existed, he or she was likely nominalist in outlook since nominalism had so long been part of the standard world view that by the 15th century in permeated the art, literature and thought of much of western Europe.

Clifford Davidson, one of the major contributors to York cycle studies, uses the name 'York Realist' to identify this supposed author while admitting to the confusion that it creates, but insists that it is still useful in that it associates the playwright with the 'realism' of the Northern painters of the late Medieval period who made similar use of detail in their work (*Creation* 117-8). Davidson admits, however, that this use of detail is akin to the experiential epistemology of nominalism rather than *philosophical realism*, which is reductionist rather than concerned with details (*Creation* 122). And, indeed, the nominalist temperament of the late Middle Ages was a reaction against philosophical realism. There is great confusion in using a term to mean one thing when it can easily be misunderstood as its opposite. The problem is compounded by the common meaning today of 'realism' and 'realistic' that is akin to the 'realism' of photography and the bold experientialism of the nineteenth century. Stanley Kahrl, who has produced the most complete critique of the name 'York Realist,' writes:

> When it appears, the term 'realism' is used without definition, the reader, it is assumed, sharing the critic's own sense of what it means. What is assumed is the meaning given to the term by the school of French Realists of the later nineteenth century, writers such as Flaubert and Zola . . . . For such writers realism [. . .] is characterized by an insistence that the writer's task was to record the data of sense impressions, verifiable in common experience, as the only reality which can be known . . . . No work of medieval literature belongs to this school of writing . . . . No writer of medieval drama [. . .] is concerned to reproduce the concrete details of medieval life, pleasant or unpleasant, as the only commonly shared area of experience knowable to his audience and himself. (72-3)

Modern 'realism' insists on a transhistorical, transcultural human experience accessible through rational inquiry. Nominalism, however, denies all universals in favor of a critical epistemology. In this sense nominalism is much more akin to post-modern cultural theory than to the ethnocentric views of the 19th and early 20th centuries. If nominalism informs the use of detail in the drama, as Davidson himself suggests, then it cannot represent a modern commonality of experience.

In *Drama and Art* Davidson notes that the movement from philosophical 'realism' to artistic 'realism,' spurred by philosophical nominalism, reaffirmed the long held view that icons lead to the contemplation of truth, rather than directly representing truth (12). Nominalist epistemology holds that symbols represent the existence of experience and can trigger experience, but cannot themselves contain experience. This follows the epistemology of Lactantius, popular throughout the Middle Ages, that art should be active, a puzzle that leads the observer to actively produce an experience of the veiled truth represented by the husk of symbol. In such a system, then, there should not exist detail for detail's sake—the detail must stand for something more than just gratuitous local flavor.[15] However, Davidson often speaks of the playwright's use of detail in gratuitous terms: "[T]he painters and the York Realist [. . .] no longer tended to follow the older practice of eliminating the arbitrary individual detail from their work" (*Creation* 118). Yet painters and dramatists do not eliminate to create (as would a photographer with an airbrush) but create by *including* details. Also, by calling the details "arbitrary" Davidson seems to be referring to the modern sense of naturalist realism to which Kahrl objects. Davidson writes: "Seemingly irrelevant details often provide the means through which an illusion of reality may be impressed upon the imagination of the audience" (*Creation* 118). Yet, unless we go back to Rossiter's now unpopular contention that the structure of the play is a fatally flawed amalgam of radically different social perspectives we cannot see the details as both symbolic and mimetic. It is unlikely that the details in these plays are opportunistic and gratuitous, anticipating modern cosmologies or appealing to some supposed universalism. They must, then, symbolically represent some understandable element of Medieval cosmology. Resonance between these details and contemporary life would serve to enhance their symbolic value, especially when obvious anachronism is involved, rather than to negate it.

Davidson approaches a solution to the confusion when he astutely observes that the realistic details of the plays are only elements in the action, not the focus, the details being part of the means to a symbolic end, rather than a formalized end in itself:

> The realism does not have its end in itself, but in the desire to make the audience *feel* what is being presented in the playing area, for only when the Passion and Crucifixion are felt can the iconography of the tableau have its desired effect. (*Creation* 124)

Collier agrees: "But in the York plays—as in all medieval religious drama—such naturalistic effects are never an end in themselves" (47). Kolve insists that the naturalistic details are part of an effect that is wholly unrealistic by design:

> This lively contract between audience and player, this delight in the openly unreal, is at the core of the medieval experience of theater. Only in such terms could actions of such magnitude and importance be played at all. (270)

We can question whether realism that is a part of an overall effect that is very unrealistic is actually realism at all. Kahrl suggests that partial uses of realism should be referred to as 'verisimilitude':

> [L]et us follow the suggestion of Edwin H. Cady, who, writing on the subject of realism in American fiction, proposed that the term 'realism' should not be used to describe 'local, partial, even fragmentary uses of realistic effects to contribute to what will in the long run and total effect be unrealistic'. For such effects he would propose the term 'verisimilitude', reserving 'realism' for works whose total effect is to insist on the data of common-sense experience as the only subject capable of being described. (73)

'Verisimilitude' is also used to distinguish the art of the Flemish painters of the fifteenth century from the realism of Italian Renaissance art. There is a distinct difference between the theoretical underpinnings of the two schools. In *Early Netherlandish Painting*, Panofsky writes:

> [T]here was a peculiar piety which seemed to distinguish the intent of Flemish painting from the humanistic—and in a sense, more formalistic—spirit of Italian art. . . . Michelangelo is said to have remarked [. . .] that Flemish paintings would bring tears to the eyes of the devout, though these were mostly "women, young girls, clerics, nuns, and gentlefolk without much understanding for the true harmony of art." (132)

Davidson does use the term 'verisimilitude' at times, but the mixture of analysis of the dramatist's use of detail in *From Creation to Doom* makes his book an interesting source of both insight and confusion concerning the topic of realism and the York Realist:

> The portion of the York Passion for which the Realist is responsible thus utilizes realism as a *means* by which to achieve an effect. . . . Thus both verisimilitude and iconography are necessary

ingredients for the York Realist, whose goal was to produce a total response in the viewer. (97)

Yet there is no room in the representational method of these plays, nor in the epistemology of critical nominalism, for gratuitous elements that appeal to a common, universal familiarity of life. Everything in them must mediate some point of meaning. The verisimilitude, then, is iconographic as well.

What confuses critics is the unique nature of the use of verisimilitude in the York Cycle in that it seems entirely spurious to the content. In the Wakefield cycle common detail adds to slapstick comedy and to the anachronistic effects, but in the York cycle these naturalistic details are very subtle, almost ambient, something Robinson noted in his original article ("Art" 244). Kahrl, Davidson and others insist that the introduction of seemingly spurious details by the Flemish painters and the Mystery cycle dramatists is a part of the philosophical shift from realism to nominalism, but none of them demonstrate *how* these added details in the York plays function in the framework of nominalist epistemology.

What I propose, then, is that the ambient and seemingly spurious details in the plays of the York cycle represent the spurious nature of human existence and choice itself. Consistently in these plays, the words and actions of bad people are shown to be absurd, either irrelevant to the divine scheme of things or ironically incorporated into it. The epistemological message contained in this system is that human beings are free to give whatever meanings to their lives that they choose and can try to impose their meanings on others; nonetheless, outside the limited bonds of mortal affairs, these impositions of meaning have no impact on the reality of God, whose affairs roll ever forward, despite the feeble attempts of petty dictators to have things their own way. The further human action is removed from the purposes of God, the more meaningless and absurd become its attempts to weave meaning out of the chaos of possibility.

The most obvious case of the meaninglessness of human existence in the York cycle is the character of Herod. The King of Judea, he can, in the human sphere, impose his will on those around him. His word is law, but his incessant bellowing shows that his power is coercive and artificial in contrast to the calm resolve of Christ. Indeed, throughout the plays evil people (and the demons) are shown to be frantic and without order in contrast with the calm and orderly power of heaven. Davidson writes of the Harrowing of Hell play: "Hell is the inverse of all that is stable and good. Even the language of the demons is topsy-turvy" (*Creation* 145). Herod's language is similar: frantic, boisterous, and sometimes without meaning:

> I faute in my reuerant in otill moy,
> I am of fauour, loo, fairer be ferre.
> Kyte oute yugilment. Vta! Oy! Oy!
> Be any witte þat Y watte it will waxe werre.

> *Seruicia primet*,
> Such losellis and lurdaynes as þou, loo,
> *Respicias timet*,
> What þe deuyll and his dame schall Y now doo?
> (XXXI, 239-46)

According to the preface to this play in Beadle and King, Jesus before Herod is dressed in a fool's outfit, and Herod treats him as an entertaining joke (175). Christ's calm resolve, though, shows his Godly power; whereas, Herod's frenetic carping shows him to be the real fool of this play, and no doubt a source of comedy for the audience. Davidson claims that Herod's antics and invented words show individuation, a part of the 'realism' of the York Realist (*Creation* 118). I am more partial, though, to Davidson's further point: "Thereby Herod, who assumes that Jesus is mad or a fool, illustrates the ultimate foolishness of those who reject salvation" (*Creation* 118). What is presented here is not 'realism' but the unreality of the meanings human beings may create in isolation. Herod's nonsense shows him to be isolated from the whole universe, his words being embedded in no context at all. In contrast, Christ's isolation in these scenes ironically demonstrates the isolation of humanity: as God he *is* the Universal context from which any real human meaning is derived. Herod demonstrates the free will of human beings to create their own contexts of meaning and power, contexts, however, that being skewed from the reality of God, are ultimately entirely unreal.

A character does not have to be evil to show the absurdity of human meaning as is evidenced by the contrasts between the young Jesus and the Doctors in play XX. The Doctors in this play are believed to have been dressed in the costume of contemporary scholars. Stevens writes that "the scene provided a potent interpretation of the power structure that Jesus had to confront to bring forth his New Law" (*Four* 78). If this is so, then it also emphasizes the foolishness of the authorities Jesus confronted, for, as Davidson notes, their scholarly arguments are nonsense:

> Examination of the York play will show that the scholastic argumentation, which begins the first Magister's *question*, is not to be taken seriously. It is the image which is at the core of the scene which is being presented here. In a sense, the audience is intended to receive something of the flavor of a medieval argument in a university without much of the substance. (*Creation* 77)

Yet that lack of substance in their arguing inevitably resonates with the nominal meaninglessness of human reason before the authority of Heaven, even in the form of a twelve year old boy. Paul writes to the Corinthians: "Where is the wise? where is the scribe? where is the disputer of this world? hath not God made foolish the wisdom of this world?" (I Corinthians 1:20) In this play the scribes and disputers of this world indeed have shown themselves foolish before God. This play has not been assigned to the supposed "York Realist" but reveals, in a simple and overt manner, the same nominalist epistemology that plays attributed to the "Realist" offer in a subtle manner with the introduction of the small, irrelevant details of human life. The nominalist flavor is subtle, ambient, part of the often unspoken assumptions of the prevailing social cosmology rather than being part of an overt philosophical argument.

One of the best pieces of evidence Robinson offers for his defense of the "Realist" name is the subtle flavor of everyday existence that he finds in the Pilate plays. For example, the inanities of Pilate's home life are acted out:

> Pilate, his wife and her 'damsel' drink and converse graciously, their elegant talk focused on the mechanics of drinking—a veritable piece of cup-and-saucer naturalism, but at the same time an ironic portrayal of gracious but wicked living. ("Art" 238)

The irony of juxtaposing petty human concerns against the most significant acts of history is seen more poignantly in Pilate's symbolic hand washing. Davidson writes:

> Another instance which illustrates the relationship between detail and meaning occurs when the York Pilate's attendant urges him to "wasshe whill þe watir is hote" (XXXIII.443). Robinson is properly impressed by this detail. "Other medieval dramatists (and more learned exegetes, too)," he insists, "would not normally concern themselves with the temperature of the water in which Pilate washed his hands—the allegorical meaning, perhaps, but not the temperature." Yet in both philosophy and art of the early fifteenth century, the tendency of the age was toward depiction of such seemingly irrelevant details as the concern of Pilate's attendant and the temperature of the water. (*Creation* 119)

I suggest that "the relationship between detail and meaning" illustrated in this play and typical of nominalist philosophy and Northern art is the pettiness of human concerns and the skewed blindness of human perception. Pilate is about to seal Christ's fate, which will fulfill all human history, and the attendant is worried about the temperature of the water. The detail is not gratuitous—it stands for the potentially supreme irrelevancy of human thought and action. The attendant's concerns signify insignificance itself.

The attendant's focus is merely on the simple act of washing the hands. Pilate, though, understands that the action signifies something more: he is condemning a man to death. Even so, Pilate misses the intense importance of what he is truly doing. Not only is God always able to accomplish his will, despite the free willed actions of human beings, he can accomplish his will through the freely willed choices of others without interfering with their agency and without their understanding the true import of their actions. This is clearly demonstrated in the most striking play attributed to the great York playwright: The Death of Christ (XXXVI).

The Death of Christ opens with Pilate demanding that the audience pay attention to the crucifixion so that they will understand the import of the scene: "Who þat to ȝone hill wille take heede/ May se þer þe soth in his sight . . ." (16-17). Collier comments: "Pilate knows, or thinks he knows, the true significance of Christ's Passion and Crucifixion, and he asserts it with a defiant and self-vindicating assuredness . . ." (170). The 'truth' he wants everyone to see is what will happen to those who rebel against his authority. Collier points out that Christ's later address to the audience, a traditional tableaux in which he asks the audience to contemplate his sacrifice, lends "a new and more satisfying direction [. . .] to Pilate's earlier statement" (176). Those who look to Christ's atoning sacrifice will "se þer þe soth in his sight." The truth in Pilate's words, hidden even from himself, demonstrates the irrelevancy of the mighty power of life and death he wields over the populous. In contrast, Christ's true power over life and death is demonstrated in his yielding up of his spirit (257-60) and the audience's anticipation of the Resurrection to follow.

Pilate's words and actions are significant in the divine scheme, but the meanings *he* attaches to them are not. Kolve's analysis of game theory in the Passion and Resurrection plays notes the asynchronous relationship between human action and the plans of God:

> [T]here are two complementary game elements, the one gratuitous and improvisatory, apparently conceived, and necessarily acted by man, the other preordained and inescapable, God's plan made known through the prophets, in which everything goes exactly as intended. (205)

The realistic details, then, are not themselves gratuitous, but do represent something of the gratuitous nature of much of human action by showing the meaninglessness of the contexts that human beings may weave with their free will and limited minds. This attitude toward meaning arises from critical nominalism's candid confrontation with the limitations of human perception and the semiotic interrelationship of all representations of experience. Rather than labeling the supposed great York playwright by just part of the means of the effect, we should make this distinction by what these means represent: the often spurious nature of mortal endeavors and meanings. If this great playwright truly did exist, it would be sensible to reject the name the "York Realist" in favor of the name the "York Nominalist." If this playwright is a fabrication of modern criticism, we may still recognize in this debate the truth of the nominalist flavor of late Medieval life and thought, a truth so ubiquitous and ambient by the fifteenth century that we might miss it if we fail to follow Mary Douglas's lead in looking for the implicit in culture when we examine the products of its social exchanges.

In the early fourteenth century the trust in reason that had dominated scholasticism and the arts for the previous two and half centuries gave way to a reassertion of the primacy of the will and the epistemologically fallen state of human perception. The ideas of Augustine and Boethius were revived against the formalist realism of Thomas and gave impetus to the critical nominalism that dominated the later Medieval centuries. Panofsky writes that by the middle of the fourteenth century "the energies of High Scholasticism [. . .] had either been channelled into poetry and, ultimately, humanism . . . or into anti-rational mysticism through Master Eckhart and his followers" (*Gothic* 11). These opposing but related strands of human thought and activity, nominalism and mysticism, along with the art and poetry that they inspired, pervade the fourteenth century with a flurry of productivity. In the fifteenth century these two extremes of the reaction against Thomism, in Panofsky's words, "prove to be *les extremes qui se touchent* [. . .] and ultimately merge, for one glorious moment, in the painting of the great Flemings, much as they did in the philosophy of their admirer, Nicholas of Cusa . . ." (*Gothic* 19-20). Similar in nominalist and mystic qualities, and also part of that "one glorious moment," are the great Mystery dramas of fifteenth century York.

Chapter 4
Ritual Compensations

I. The Implicit Anagoge and the Ritual Identification with Deity

In the first chapter I praised Richard Emmerson's refreshing contention that typology is not the only level of allegory functioning in Medieval thought and art, and that typology, tropology and anagoge are all of equal importance. In chapter two, however, I reasserted the claim of Auerbach, Muller and others that figurative typology is the new, Christian element in Greek allegory, and as such the *raison d'etre* for a new, revitalizing cosmology. As a consequence typology is by far the most noticeable level of allegorical meaning in Medieval art, which is one reason why the word 'allegory' is often used to mean only typology (or *figura* in Auerbach's terminology) by many writers. In chapter three, I reverse myself again, arguing that all the levels of meaning are equally important since the truth of Christ's typological intervention in history cannot be understood without the Holy Spirit's tropological intervention in the individual. If I may be permitted one more reversal, I wish to assert that there is one level of allegorical meaning more important than all the others: the anagogical level.

This at first may seem illogical, since, as typology is the most used allegorical level in Medieval art and poetry, anagoge is certainly the least used, and the least understood. However, anagoge's recondite nature is a part of its very function. The anagogical level of meaning in Bonaventure's trinities is analogous to the ineffable Father and represents the union of the soul with God. The human inability, after the Fall, to directly "know" the Father is what necessitates the typology of human history and the tropology of the individual's journey through good and evil in life. It is the typology hidden in the literal events of history and the tropology hidden in the events of one's life that link the literal level of mortal experience with the eternal experience of God—and for the Medieval Christian, God is totality, the complete and all encompassing truth of which all mortal truths are but reflections that point the mind toward God the Father.

The few obviously anagogical elements in the York cycle are promises of eternal rest and reward (or hell's damnation as the case may be) that are at times presented, and most especially in the last two plays, The Coronation of the Virgin and The Last Judgment, which are entirely anagogical. However, since the very purpose of the emotional, meditative arts of late Medieval northern Europe was to lead the soul to an experience of truth, of unity with the divine, anagoge is implicitly present in every phrase, every icon, every gesture in the entire cycle. Indeed, the York cycle itself can be seen as a massive and necessarily anagogical representation of the existence and will of God. The cycle dramatizes Christ's life, but by doing so, it forms a testimony of the Father, and the way given to know the Father. Christ is the focus of cultural meaning, and so his is by far the largest role in the drama (as typology has the largest role in allegory), but everything about his dramatic actions, and all the other action as well, speaks of the Father who can only be known through Christ and the Holy Ghost.

Why are these esoteric religious questions so important? And could they have been so important to ordinary Medieval people? Williams argues that any critic using typology to explain Medieval plays must be able to show how the typological metaphor was explicitly conveyed in simple, obvious, and most importantly, theatrical means (680). He would no doubt be more critical of the use of anagoge to explain the plays, which is even less susceptible to explicit representation. Yet an important foundation of Mary Douglas's theory of cultural anthropology is the insistence that most cultural meaning is implicit and obliquely cued (*Implicit* 3-4).[16] Cultural critics, then, must immerse themselves in the culture under study in order to identify the implicit. It is perhaps difficult to identify implicit meanings from oblique cultural cues, but understanding any human culture inevitably demands a high level of complex contextualizing.

Interestingly, the epistemological task of the cultural interpreter (in Douglas's eyes) is markedly similar to the active epistemology of Medieval representation: human meanings always entail active interpretation where the transference of symbols leads to the identification of meaning within an implicit cultural context. Robertson, noting the popularity of Lactantius's epistemology of poetry, writes: "Thus, in Petrarch's quotations from Lactantius, he is made to say that poets transfer 'those things which are true' rather than 'actual occurrences'" (*Preface* 345). Human experience is never transparent. The "truth" in any occurrence, no matter how simplified or explicitly expressed, resides in implied meanings, in the cosmology of the culture, which in Douglas's terms consists of "the ultimate justifying ideas which tend to be invoked as if part of the natural order and yet which [. . .] are evidently not at all natural but strictly a product of social interaction" ("Grip/Group" 5). There is no meaning in human experience outside of cultural contexts.

The seemingly esoteric explanation from Medieval theology of the literal, typological, tropological and anagogical levels of meaning in the York cycle are important, then, because they reflect an implied cosmology. These levels of significance are part of the culture's construction of meaning. The anagoge implicit in the drama parallels the anagoge implicit in the cosmology of the culture. These questions, then, go to the heart of the culture. Indeed, it is in this anagogical level of meaning that we find a clue to the productivity of the ritual compensations in the societies of late Medieval northern Europe.[17]

Classical Europeans were no strangers to mystical unity with deity. The pantheism at the heart of Classical thought easily allows for mystical identification with deity, and the Greek drama, being a product of Dionysian ritual, was heavy in God/Human unification symbolism. Christian cosmology, though, if it is to resist pantheism (and dualism) must insist that, though God's power and will informs every facet of creation, he is entirely separate from his creation.[18] On a ritual level this complicates the mystical identification with deity because a human being cannot truly be one with God the Father in the mortal state, hence the need for salvation mediated by Christ, and illumination mediated by the Holy Spirit. The events in the play of The Transfiguration (XXIII) attest to the incompatibility of the mortal and eternal states: Christ in the mortal state must be transfigured to commune with heavenly messengers; the apostles in the same play are invited to but cannot achieve this same transfiguration.

The nominalists of late Medieval Europe emphasized the multiplicity of forms and the tentativeness of human knowing; whereas their mystic contemporaries emphasized the radical otherness of God and the need for "the self-extinction of the human soul in God" (Panofsky, *Gothic* 15). These two dominant strains of late Medieval thought interact in the York cycle in an attempt to achieve a mystical identification with God with ritual efficacy for the community. For pantheism the deity is continually available, completely inseparable from the natural world, including one's own body. For the Medieval Christian, the natural world, being God's creation, is a key to understanding God, but it is not a direct experience of God. The Medieval need for identification with deity is more urgent than in the Classical period, while at the same time it has become more difficult. For Medieval Christian cosmology, then, God's extreme otherness and humanity's inability to directly know (or possess) God threatens to cast humanity adrift in its own pettiness, unanchored in the certainty the deity offers.

The tentativeness of late Medieval thought is as frightening as it is exhilarating. Many have seen the use of added detail in the plays as functioning with the pervasive anachronism to legitimize the audience's life experience. My argument in the previous chapter that the nominalist function of the detail does not affirm the human experience, but rather accuses it of potential irrelevance, might seem to be a humanistically sterile reading, but only if seen out of context. Although these plays dramatized the historical perspective, the producers of the cycle did not care to glorify the drama of mortal history, but rather they showed a great concern to raise the audience's temporal minds to the Eternal Truth. This can be seen in another late Medieval text, *Sir Gawain and the Green Knight*, in which the human space in the story is less real than the mystical space.[19] The late Medieval "delight in the openly unreal" (271) that Kolve notes is a product of the Medieval definition of humanity and the world in contrast with God and the heavens. As I have argued, though, these cultural definitions are primarily epistemological and function to locate the human experience within the framework of epistemological possibilities. This human space, as Gawain also discovers, is uncomfortable, unfulfilling, restless, and uncertain. The blatantly iconographic, stylized nature of Medieval art reflects a recognition of the limited, reductionist nature of all human cognition. Many modern minds see the representational methods of Medieval art and drama as simple and naive, but from the Medieval perspective, modern realism would seem simple and naive in its belief that experience yields up a transparent reality and in its eschewing of anagogical themes.

Not only is the mystical identification with deity more urgent and more complicated in the Medieval world than in the Classical, it is potentially more dangerous, more likely to be considered blasphemy, and, indeed, from the beginning of the cycle plays there were detractors among the Lollards and others who vigorously opposed them as dangerously blasphemous. In order to be so bold as to represent divine things and attempt ritual efficacy on such a new and grand scale, especially in the context of the nominalist and mystic sentiments of the day, the York cycle had to highlight the utter separation of humanity from deity as well as to offer a ritual unity with deity.

Humanity's need to identify with deity and its unworthiness to do so are made most explicit in the Last Judgment play in exactly the place where the deity reaches out in identification with humanity by asking after the corporal acts of mercy as occurs at the end of the twenty-fifth chapter of Matthew. Since humanity is fallen and unworthy of grace, the mystical identification with the deity must be offered by the deity. Christ identifies himself with all who suffer in his address to the good *animae* on his right:

> Whenne I was hungery ჳe me fedde,
> To slake my thirste youre harte was free;
> Whanne I was clothles ჳe me cledde,
> Ჳe wolde no sorrowe vppon me see.
> In hard presse whan I was stedde,
> Of my payns ჳe hadde pitee;
> Full seke whan I was brought in bedde,
> Kyndely ჳe come to coumforte me.
> (XLVII, 285-92)

Later Christ declares the opposite case to the bad *animae* on his left: When in need they cast him out and despised him. They respond with feeble defenses, the first asking: "Whan had þou, þat all thing has,/ Hunger or thirste, sen þou God is?" (XLVII, 349-50) This *anima* does not believe that God can suffer. *II Anima Mala* says: "Whan was it we saw þe seke, allas?/ Whan kid we þe þis vnkyndenesse?" (XLVII, 353-4) Both bad souls have ignored God's identification with humanity through the incarnation of Christ, and so they do not see the neglect of God in the neglect of human suffering. Their answers are petty defenses and represent their ignorance of what is truly important. Yet, the good *animae* answer Christ's earlier statement to them in a similar way:

> *I Anima Bona*
> Whanne hadde we, lorde þat all has wroght,
> Meete and drinke þe with to feede,
> Sen we in erþe hadde neuere noght
> But thurgh þe grace of thy Godhede?
> *II Anima Bona*
> Whanne waste þat we þe clothes brought,
> Or visite þe in any nede,
> Or in þi sikenes we þe sought?
> Lorde, when did we þe þis dede?
> (XLVII, 301-8)

Though their responses are similar to those of the bad *animae*, the responses of the good *animae* obviously represent humility, not defense. In contrast to their humility, the responses of the bad *animae* show their arrogance: they believe they would have known God and recognizing him would have served him. The good *animae* humbly question whether, indeed, they have committed worthy deeds. In Luke's words, even when we have fulfilled all commands, yet "[w]e are unprofitable servants" to the Omnipotent (Luke 17:10). The deeds of the good *animae* make them worthy because the grace of the forgiving God declares it to be so.

This final judgment is the ultimate anagoge in the cosmology, representing the completed state of all the characters. Yet, this judgment is mystically always present in the eyes of the Eternal God and represents the Eternal disposition, and therefore the Eternal truth, of all things. The ending anagoge is present throughout the cycle in the form of the ritual invoking of God's identification with humanity. However, this identification is presented in a dramatic structure that constantly highlights the representational process in a respectfully humble acknowledgment of humanity's limited abilities to represent anagogical truths. The cycle unifies the audience with God by engaging it in a representation of history from God's perspective—the audience, then, is constructed as God! This is represented in two ways: 1) All time is seen in one complete viewing, beginning and ending in Eternity (the Boethian cosmology discussed in Chapter

Three). 2) The subjects of the plays are the significant events of history from the divine, rather than the worldly, perspective.

On the other hand the audience identification with deity is continually broken in three ways: 1) By the discrete nature of the structure—the periods between pageants inevitably break up the presentation of the material, and thereby include periods in which the audience's focus is away from the storyline. 2) By the overt use of stylized, iconographic representations, that continually insists that what is being presented is allegorical, not realistic. 3) By the ubiquitous use of the traditional modes of audience address that temporarily break the narrative attitude, and momentarily shifting the construction of the audience to its temporal context, incorporate that context into the action.   These breaks in the representational process serve both mystical purposes by offering an identification with God and a recognition of his radical otherness.   They ritualize the identification with Deity in the plays by directly incorporating the audience, but they also remind the audience that what they are seeing is representational. The images and speeches do not truly reproduce the experience of God, which is not possible within the limitations of human epistemology, but following Lactantius's husk and kernel epistemology, they might help one to a personal experience of God through the allegorical representation of God's will as manifested in human history.

Incorporating the audience by breaking the mimetic process, or by overtly pointing to its functions and limitations, serves a major role in the ritual functions of the cycle.   According to Robinson these forms of direct address were traditional in Medieval drama, and the "York Realist" and "Wakefield Master" took full advantage of them (*Studies* 27). He writes further that "[t]he York Realist acknowledges the presence of the audience by his direct addresses to them when, as usual, they become both onlookers and characters. . ." (*Studies* 52). Most of the direct addresses (but not all) are in the form of closing benedictions in which one of the characters offers a traditional parting blessing to the audience. These blessings offer a variety of ways to acknowledge both the action and the audience and usually begin as part of the action directed to other characters and then incorporate a rhetorical glance at the audience, who are thereby brought into the action.

86

An important example of direct address is the last speech of the play of Christ's Appearance to Mary Magdalene (XXXIX):

> *Jesus*
> To Galile schall þou wende
> Marie, my doghtir dere,
> Vnto my brethir hende,
> þer þei are all in fere.
> Telle þame ilke worde to ende
> þat þou spake with me here.
> Mi blissing on þe lende,
> And all þat we leffe here.
> (XXXIX, 142-9)

Sometimes an ending blessing can be seen as entirely a part of the action, such as the parting blessing that Jesus gives to his Apostles at the end of the play of The Incredulity of Thomas (XLI). In these cases the incorporation of the audience is obliquely implied by its parallelism with other such blessings, or perhaps cued by the actor turning his head toward the audience. Other plays, especially in the Passion sequence, call for a mob to be present and the use of direct address makes the audience a part of it. In the play of Christ's Appearance to Mary Magdalene, however, the "all þat we leffe here" can only be acknowledging the audience, since there is no-one else in the garden with the Magdalene and Christ. Any acknowledgment of others present, then, serves to break the actor's role and the play's action in acknowledgment of the audience's context. These breaks overtly point to the "unreality" of the presentation—it is only a representation, and the actor, by acknowledging the audience where no audience is called for in the action, reminds himself and the audience that he is only an actor, a mere human being humbly representing deity.

This is a histrionic form of stylizing which actively resists the lure of "naturalism" in a manner similar to the iconographic, stylized representations of contemporary visual art. In this way late Medieval artists could use verisimilitude and still convey the message that ultimate truth is not transparent to the literal experience of mortal beings. Audience address, then, is part of the self-revealing structure of the plays, which represents a nominalist tentativeness toward epistemology. However, this tentativeness, rather than undermining the authority of the meanings presented, serves to emphasize the communal production of those meanings as the character turns to the audience and once again becomes the actor serving his role in the ritual in which they have all had some part. The acknowledgment of the audience, then, is also a reaching out for acknowledgment from the audience, for a communal confirmation of the tentative communication of the play.

Collier writes that "[a]lmost two-thirds of the York plays end with some such explicit acknowledgment of the audience from the stage" (195). Often a similar address to the audience occurs at the beginning of the play also, and with the benediction, forms a frame for the episode, starting in the audience's context, presenting a representation of an episode embedded in an Eternal context, and then returning to the audience's context. Collier says this "confirms the present relevance of the historical scene" (196). Such didactic purposes, though, cannot be primary, since no-one in the audience would likely doubt the relevance of sacred history. Collier himself notes the familiarity of the idea that "the events of the plays are relevant to the audience since the will of God that so clearly informs them informs all moments in time. . . " (193). A more significant role of this framing of individual plays is to set the present in epistemological context, overtly recognizing the limits of human perception and attempting to ritually compensate for the real gap between the context of the present and past contexts from which present culture has arisen. Further, the framing around episodes grants them a microcosmic resonance to the framing of the whole cycle, which encourages the audience to see its own context in an Eternal perspective.

Collier writes that some opening speeches are not addressed directly to the audience but are spoken generally (197). Most notably, the lines of God (the Father) are always general, "as if to confirm His essential sublimity" (197). This generality of speaking helps indicate that the representation of God is anagogical, and indicates that he is, in effect, addressing the whole of Creation. These addresses by God are important and interesting breaks in the audience's perspective of seeing history from God's view. Whenever God speaks in the cycle the audience is momentarily shifted from having God's Eternal perspective to being the world instructed by God, or better stated, by another human being that is here performing Gaytryge's epistemological "leryinge" while the audience is "heryinge," radically testifying to the representational nature of the art and the

88

communal nature of the anagoge. In these instances the audience oscillates between being like God viewing the world and being the world instructed by God. The *theatrum mundi* of the late Medieval period, then, is also a *theatrum Dei*, an anagoge of God and a construction of the world as one community of God's creation. This fits well into the demands of the Corpus Christi celebration since a communal and anagogical experience is precisely what is called for in Urban IV's Bull *Transiturus* of 1264, renewed by Clement V in 1311, which established the festival of Corpus Christi. Collier writes:

> The liturgy for the Feast of Corpus Christi in particular aims at creating a communion in joy, an intention which the Papal bull first proposing the Feast clearly defines: "It is for this reason that on the same Thursday the devout crowds of the faithful should flock eagerly to the Churches—in order that clergy and congregation, joining one another in equal rejoicing, may rise in a song of praise, and then, from the hearts and desires, from the mouths and lips of all, there may sound forth hymns of joy at man's salvation." (146)

Music itself is a supreme representation of heavenliness for the culture that produced these plays. Nan Cooke Carpenter's work with the music of the Wakefield Master's *Secunda Pastorum* hints at music's anagogical content by contrasting the Angel's song with the good shepherds' humble imitation of it, and the sinful Mak's inability to be musical at all (697-9). Joy, as well, is an anagogical emotion, the human parallel of God's experience. The idea, then, of communal hymns of joy has an inescapable anagogical resonance; indeed, to be a part of such an experience would certainly have mystical potential in the sacred system context of late Medieval England. As a later extension of this ritual impulse toward public singing in praise of the Incarnation, the Mystery dramas naturally anticipate the participation of the entire community in the production of cultural meaning. The incorporation of the audience into the action, then, is not an invention of the mystery drama, but represents a cultural impulse that the drama, when it came along, had to satisfy. This indicates that the techniques used to incorporate the audience, such as direct address (and its several potential perspective shifts), the use of familiar liturgical elements, pervasive but always meaningful anachronisms, and so on, grew up with the drama as an integral part of its structure and evolution. They are solutions to existing demands, not tacked on innovations.

The most overt ritualizing of the very activity of presenting mystery plays occurs at the end of the play of The Supper at Emmaus, as many critics have noted. In explaining the haste of their departure, *I Perigrinus* makes specific reference to the cycle's process:

> Here may we notte melle more at þis tyde,
> For prossesse of plaies þat precis in plight.
> He bringe to his blisse on euery ilke side,
> þat sofferayne lorde þat moste is of might.
> (XL, 191-4)

Collier notes that "for modern readers, used to self-enclosed and internally consistent fiction," this reference to the process of plays "may well seem slightly comical," but argues that for the Medieval audience this was "an economical and vivid way" to point out that the truth of the Resurrection is timeless (Collier 195). Collier's reference to modern expectations is apt. The seamlessness of modern realistic narrative reflects a desire to eschew the ritualizing tendencies in literature. F. C. Gardiner in his thematic treatise *The Pilgrimage of Desire*, interprets this speech of *I Perigrinus* as an essential expression of the ritual function of the cycle drama:

> Still rooted in the ritualizing impulse of religious drama, this York play sees in the other episodes in the cycles a context of successive moments of insight. The very knowledge of plays already seen in the cycle and of the process of plays yet to come, assures the York audience of a universe in which pilgrimage will evolve along the successive stages of an achieved transcendence. (147)

For much of late modern drama the audience consists of detached observers granted a privileged perspective on the action of the play. The Medieval audience is an integral part of the action of the York mystery cycle, and this inclusion of the audience grants a communal, ritualized dimension to the plays.

This ritual dimension was a natural level of cultural participation for the Medieval audience, who were, as William Munson writes, "accustomed to processional ceremony" (192). Ashley states that ritualized theatrics were of the utmost importance to the ceremonial life of Medieval Europe:

> From the fourteenth through the sixteenth centuries, virtually every communal event was marked by costumed processions, mimed tableaux, and plays. . . . What we now call drama [. . .] may more usefully be considered cultural performance, something to be studied as part of the ritual and the ceremony of late medieval society. (57)

The urgent necessity for the identification with deity is underscored by the structure and message of the cycle, for the attempt to ritually compensate for the otherness of God emphatically testifies to that awful otherness. The tentativeness in the structure suggests the tentativeness in all human communication and understanding. But rather than undermining itself, the self-critical honesty of the cycle's self-interrogating structure is a powerful appeal for the absolute necessity of both the nominalist theme, by emphasizing the communal production of meaning, and the mystical theme, by emphasizing the need to invoke an epistemologically enlightening identification with the divine. This communal invoking of deity and cosmology is the foundation of culture—and the York cycle beautifully lays bare this process in an intricately rich display of cultural introspection and production.

II. The Ritual Recovery of the Past

Richard Homan in his stimulating article "Ritual Aspects of the York Cycle" says that the ritual efficacy of the cycle resides in the incorporation of the audience through anachronism, and that Kolve was correct in arguing that this incorporation compensates the audience for the insignificance of their position in salvation history (306). However, the historical moment of the audience could not have been represented as insignificant in the cosmology of the culture. Since in Medieval culture the world and all its history is a product of God's will, there is no room in the cosmology for an insignificant period of history, not even the post-meridian age. It is only the action of individuals, lost in the epistemological limitations of mortality, that can attain insignificance by constructing meanings skewed from God's will, but the cycle warns against this confusion rather than ritually compensating for it. Homan further argues that the significance of typology, which Auerbach revealed, provides the means for anachronism to take on ritual power (307). I believe typology's coloring of history is indeed a key to the ritual efficacy of the cycle, but that it compensates for the general limitations of human beings to perceive truth (reflected in typology's divine interpretation of history) rather than compensating for anything specific to the post-meridian age.

Following the analysis of Anthony Graham-White and referencing further the work of the anthropologist Victor Turner, Homan argues that ritual must be sufficient to bring about the resolution of some real conflict in the social construction of the culture (305). Principles of social organization must be at stake:

> Turner sees this resolution of incompatible claims among the principles on which a social structure depends as part of the ritual process. Without such resolution, the society must fall into disorder and undergo some actual revolution. (309)

Homan discovered at least one economically significant ritual function of the drama, to ritually compensate for the lopsidedness of guild power in York where the Mercers guild dominated the power structure. Homan writes:

> The political system here is apparently open to all trades: no trade is by definition superior, and none are excluded. Yet, Sellers identifies six members of the Twelve and seven members of the Twenty-Four as Mercers (v. 120, pp. viii-ix), and [. . .] especially in the fifteenth century, the Mercers achieved a very powerful position by purchasing lands through their religious fraternity, and [. . .] controlling the city council. . . . The distribution of political power among the guilds and groups of guilds is balanced to suggest representation of all, but in fact to concentrate power in the hands of the Mercers. (311)

Homan points out, though, that this seeming "tyranny" in what is supposed to be a democratic structure is actually a circumstantial necessity for the continued success of the community, hence the need for ritual compensation of this social "anomaly" (311-2).

Though this compensating for the lopsided guild power structure is essential to the smooth operation of the community, Homan notes that this ritualized resolution of the power structure is probably not the major ritual purpose of the cycle, that it was a "logical continuation of the ritual purpose revealed by the internal evidence of the event" (314-5). The citizens of York used the ritual efficacy of the cycle's annual production for this purpose because the cycle was already the focus of community ritual. And, indeed, I have proposed that one central ritual function for the York cycle is the need to resolve the conflict between the radical otherness of God and the need to be united with God. By interrogating the culturally defining contrasts between humanity and Deity, the ritual underscores the epistemological need for human beings to possess and pass on knowledge. Since the deity is the root of all cultural meanings in a sacred system context, the identification of the attributes of God, and the discovery of means by which human beings may commune with God, must be the central focus of ritual life. These rituals invoke the basic cosmology of the culture and the epistemological potential of human beings within that cosmology. The economic impact of the ritual goes to the heart of human economics: the representation and transmittal of cultural knowledge. The York cycle, then, represents the mythos at the heart of the culture.

Kathleen Ashley writes that Medieval dramas are best defined as "cultural performances" which are "occasions on which a society dramatizes its collective myths, defines itself and reflects on its practices and values" (57). From this perspective the mystery cycle serves a ritual purpose similar to epic poetry in its oral, communal state. Minna Skafte Jensen in "The Homeric Epics and Greek Cultural Identity" states well the cultural value of epic:

> The epic [. . .] is a very important genre for maintaining cultural identity, precisely because it ties the present to the past and thus supplies the listeners with a feeling that they share their culture with former generations. At the same time, the very broadness of the narrative enables the poet to encompass whatever is considered typical of the group concerned: its way of life, political and

religious practices, material surroundings, etc., and to introduce a
great variety of persons to set good or bad examples. (36)

The York cycle performs these same normative functions for the community that
produced it as an annual communal enterprise. However, rather than the hero
being a cultural ancestor, the hero of the Corpus Christi cycle is Christ, who
successfully battles the forces of evil and offers society solutions to its moral and
epistemological struggles. If we see the York cycle as having a cultural
productivity parallel to that of epic poetry, we can see another important ritual
function of the cycle: to compensate for the temporality of human existence.

God, in the Boethian model, possesses all time at once, whereas human
beings have only the moment. Human beings, then, are lost in the segmentation
of time and their limited, temporal perspective. There is a "Mystical Unity of
Time" presented in the York cycle (often represented by the use of anachronism),
but the very need to formulate such a unity reveals the true and inescapable linear
separation of the years and generations. And this, indeed, goes to the heart of
human existence: human beings succeed by colonizing on the information passed
on to them by preceding generations. The epistemological problems of the
Mystery drama, then, is a variation of the perennial human problem: how to
represent truth so that it can be successfully communicated to others and down
through the generations.

The basic solution to the need to transmit meaning is the superdialect of
symbols of the culture, but our temporality means that contexts continually
change resulting in new qualitative meanings as well as new quantities.
Recovering the significant qualitative experiences of the past from their semiotic
remains is an impossibly difficult task of contextualizing since the context of past
experience cannot truly be reconstructed; nonetheless, the attempt to recover the
past can yield significant clues to the qualities of past events, their contexts, and
their significance to present contexts. Beneath the surface operations of the
Christian mythology of the cycle are the implications of a thousand years of
cultural development in Western Europe—a record of the cultural solutions that
we recognize as the distinct flavor of Medieval culture as manifested in the
particular context of late Medieval York.

Collier quotes Axton's assertion that the vernacular drama resists the time-arresting abstractions of the liturgy such as "Gregorian chant, ecclesiastical costume, setting and ceremonial action" in favor of incorporating contemporary experience into sacred history, and says that the popular use of the vernacular for religious drama marks "a basic change in medieval spirituality" (50-1). It also represents a shift of spiritual power and meaning from residing only with the guardians of these time-arresting liturgical symbols to residing in a communal context. Spiritual meaning becomes the product and property of the entire community rather than being imposed by established hierarchies. Collier notes the democratic dimension to the incorporation of the audience into religious drama:

> The Corpus Christi drama makes no attempt to exclude its audience as a later, more "realistic" drama might. Nor on the other hand, does it assume the participation of its audience as the liturgical drama, as part of the ritual of the church, can do. In a variety of ways, more often subtle than overt, the Corpus Christi drama acknowledges its audience to elicit and direct its involvement in what it sees and hears. (17)

By incorporating contemporary society into the ritualized past, but also overtly pointing to the reality that the drama is a piece of contemporary life representing the past, the drama ritually resolves the conflict of the culture's need for the past while only having the here and now. This ritually compensates for the perspective shifts necessitated by the constant changes of temporal existence: the epistemological need of culture to both transmit knowledge and change as context changes.

The annual repetition of the event grants society an opportunity for cultural introspection and shifts of perspective—a necessity of temporality, and in obvious contrast to the singularity of the divine events the cycle celebrates. Like the repetition of figures in the Old Testament plays, or the repetition of animal sacrifice in ancient Hebrew traditions, the temporal need for the ritual repetition of these cycles demonstrates by contrast the divine efficacy of Christ's singular sacrifice. Paul writes to the Hebrews:

> For the law having a shadow of good things to come, and not the very image of the things, can never with those sacrifices which they offered year by year continually make the comers thereunto perfect. For then would they not have ceased to be offered? . . . For by one offering he hath perfected for ever them that are sanctified. (Hebrews 10:1-2, 14)

God's will is singular in purpose and his actions entirely efficacious, but fallen human beings need a continual affirmation of faith. On the simplest level of ritual efficacy, then, these plays are an annual public affirmation of faith in a religious context that grants sufficient ritual power to the free willed confession of faith in the divinity of events far in the past.

Stevens suggests that the anachronistic incorporation of the audience in the Mystery drama has the potential to enlighten our own understanding of dramatic representation, and that those who seek to re-create the literal Medieval experience of the plays in our own time violate the ritual spirit of the plays:

> Even an examination of the phenomenon of performance proper can add to our understanding of anachronism as a dramatic principle. When, for example, a company re-creates a medieval play in its historic setting—presenting the play on a pageant wagon, re-creating the medieval marketplace as a stage, using medieval costumes—does it defy the spirit of the play? Is not such a performance exactly what the play itself warns against? The original medieval productions did not re-create biblical settings, so why should modern performances re-create medieval settings (except perhaps as a classroom exercise)? ("Medieval" 48)

This book is itself driven by this basic human paradox of needing the past but being unable to truly retain or recover it. We cannot recreate the milieu of fifteenth-century York, nor the festival context of the plays, nor the religious fervor of the period in modern revivals of the cycle any more than the cycle in its day could reproduce the context of ancient Palestine. Yet just as the plays create a symbolic compensation for the loss of the past that might lead a fifteenth-century citizen of York to a personal experience of the cultural truth of the Corpus Christi story, we can, with our own critical reconstructions, discover clues to the implicit cosmology in the late Medieval York cycle that might lead us to personal experiences of the cosmological coherence and epistemological aesthetics of late Medieval culture.

In its day the mystery cycle was a new and productive form of literature, the beginning of a new cultural context. Stevens writes of the cycle drama:

> At least in England, they are probably the most important literary works of their times, even if they are not the expression of the elite. They combine with the works of Thomas Malory, the other great literary accomplishment of fifteenth-century England, to define a new social order. Theirs is the matrix of the new; Malory's the tragic-heroic reflection of the old. ("Medieval" 46)

In the early fifteenth-century the mature York cycle was a bold and exciting perspective on the human experience, but like the typology it used, it drew its strength from being embedded in the ancient traditions of the culture—a formula that, like typology, offered a solution to the cultural need to respond to contemporary contexts while retaining the wisdom of the past. In the last forty years of our own era these plays have become new and exciting again as light has been thrown on their rare beauty, a beauty missed earlier through a lack of understanding of the structure of social cosmology and epistemology of late Medieval societies. The true beauty of the York cycle, in its day as in ours, is found in the reflection it offers of the society that created it as a ritual representation of itself.

NOTES

Introduction

1. See, for example, Butler 366.

Chapter One

2. All quotes to the York cycle are taken from *The York Plays*, edited by Richard Beadle (1982).

3. By making this comparison between Moon and the representational methods of the earlier drama I do not mean to disparage the medium in any way. Though Shakespeare may be poking fun at the simple representational dramatics of Moon, his art is of a higher degree, but not a different type. Moon's crudeness and naiveté represent an exaggeration of the human epistemological condition from the traditional Medieval perspective, having the ability to represent knowledge, but only through semiotic mediation. Shakespeare is poking fun at humankind's epistemological crudeness at the same time he is celebrating humanity's nonetheless fantastically rich potential to fashion reality with these simple, mortal representations.

4. Beadle calls the first play The Fall of the Angels and the second play The Creation. Collier (whose book predates Beadle's edition) is using more traditional titles. Davidson prefers the titles from the Index of the Records of Early English Drama (Johnston & Rogerson) "since these reproduce more exactly the titles as they are extant in an early fifteenth-century list" (*Creation* ix). However, Davidson does prefer Beadle's numbering of the plays and provides an appendix aligning Beadle's numbering to the traditional titles (*Creation* 229-32). In the Index, I list plays by Beadle's number and the guild associated with each play without reference to either titling system.

Chapter Two

5. See, for example, Davidson, *Creation* Ch. 3, Collier pp. 159, 208-211, Kolve Ch. 4, and Meyers's article.

98

6. One possible exception to this model is The Saddlers' Play—The Harrowing of Hell, if Hell resides in Eternity. But Eternity, by Boethian definition, is God's perspective, a state of complete goodness. The Earth and Hell are below Heaven because they are sinful states. This common Medieval ordering of the cosmos is established by God in stanza four of the first play: "Here vndernethe me nowe a nexile I neuen,/ Whilke ile sall be erthe. Now all be at ones/ Erthe haly, and helle, þis hegheste be heuen. . ." (I, 25-27). As well, in The Harrowing of Hell, Adam, speaking to the souls in Hell, says, "Foure thowsande and sex hundreth yere/ Haue we bene heere in þis stedde" (XXXVII, 39-40). This indicates that Hell is subject to time, and, therefore, separate from Eternity.

7. For evidence in favor of this staging, see Collier 250, 257; Davidson 188; Johnston & Rogerson 55.

Chapter Three

8. See Mary Douglas's description of the Grid / Group quadrants in "Cultural Bias" (205-26) and her analysis of the contradictions inherent in Low Grid (238-46).

9. Healy's commentary here is almost a direct translation of *Breviloquium* Prl. 4, t.V. Following the Latin usage, Healy uses the word 'allegory' to mean 'typology' rather than all four levels, a common practice in older texts.

10. Kolve's footnote to this idea is Thoresby's *The Lay Folks' Catechism* (8-18). Such popular references testify to the widespread understanding of these seemingly esoteric notions concerning the limits of human knowledge.

11. Stevens says the regynalls were compiled sometime between 1432 and 1468, with the early 1440s as his best guess (49). Robinson dates the work of the "York Realist" as "some decades before 1463--but probably not before 1422," and probably "early in the middle third of the fifteenth century" (*Studies* 19).

12. Knowles writes:

> [T]hose who prize the intellectual and religious achievements of thirteenth century scholasticism have often in the past found in Ockham and Nominalism what some have found to-day in Marx and Communism, the fount and source of all that is ill done. In both cases [. . .] the complex of ideas and tendencies is far too wide for any 'ism' to contain, and an individual, however great his genius, is always a representative and an heir as well as being an originator. We must beware, therefore, of regarding Ockham as

responsible for all the philosophical and theological agnosticism that came after him. (325)

Panofsky is careful to differentiate Ockham's *critical* nominalism from the dogmatic nominalism of Roscellinus (*Gothic* 12).

13. Again, note the defense of productive cultural relativisms from Mary Douglas ("Grid/Group" 2) and Clifford Geertz (234) referenced in the Introduction to this book (1-3).

14. Perhaps even the much maligned Roscellinus has been unfairly accused of superficiality. Knowles notes that he was reacting against the almost ridiculously reductionist tendencies of the eleventh century's extreme realism, and that "many of those who attacked him, or subsequently wrote of him, understood his nominalism in a less subtle, more radical sense" (Knowles 111).

15. There is a distinct difference between the iconography of the Romanesque and the Gothic periods, but it is essentially a qualitative difference, the basic quantities remaining constant and supplemented by the emergence of many more due to the pluralist tendencies of nominalism. The mediating function of representation, however, remained. Davidson points out that the thickening of the dramatic scenes in late Medieval art through the addition of detail and perspective was "an extension of the tentativeness introduced through philosophical nominalism" (*Drama* 12), but that the resulting productions do not alter the iconographic import of the scenes:

> The conservative nature of drama is proof of its derivative character; it is rarely innovative with regard to either iconography or ways of visualizing scenes. The art hence provided, as we have seen, models for the crucial moments within the cycle plays, which only require the "fleshing out" of scenes by means of action and dialogue. (*Drama* 13)

This suggests that the drama is itself a way to enrich the iconography. Robertson notes Chaucer's similar enriching of iconography through the considerable use of verisimilitude and the appearance of "new iconographic motifs [. . .] which are either elaborations of old ones, or details whose meanings are supplied by the contexts in which they appear" (*Preface* 242).

100

Chapter Four

16. Mary Douglas's theory of the implicit deals with the unconscious backgrounding of information that is either in conflict with other essential information, or constitutes

> the necessary unexamined assumptions upon which ordinary discourse takes place. . . . [A] large part of discourse is dedicated to creating, revising and obliquely affirming this implicit background, without ever directing explicit attention upon it. (*Implicit* 4)

On a simpler level, implied knowledge of the myth is essential to the meaning of much of the drama, as Ross discovered for the *Secunda Pastorum*. An example from the York cycle can be found in the play of The Flight into Egypt (XIX). After finding the solution to their lost state (they do not know the road to Egypt) by placing faith in the Christ child in their arms, Joseph and Mary set off in confidence to Egypt. A cultural outsider might ask if they do ever make it to Egypt. The knowledge of their eventual success is a given on which the drama's message of their problem and its resolution is based.

17. Homan notes the consensus of several cultural critics

> that ritual cannot be distinguished by appearances alone, but the cultural context, or *context of beliefs*, provides a frame of reference within which a certain performance has either primarily aesthetic value, and hence is primarily dramatic, or is of greater *efficacy*. . . . (304)

Homan further notes that ritual efficacy indicates "that the performance is both efficient and *sufficient* in producing its result. . ." (305). Ritual performs the actual work of social and cultural repair:

> [W]hen Shaw or Brecht says that a play should change the world, we understand that he means a play should motivate people to work for change; we do not suspect either of supposing that at the end of a performance things have been set right. This, however, is exactly what ritual supposes. While propaganda and art may be efficient in bringing about change, ritual is sufficient, insofar as the participants are concerned. (305)

Homan follows Victor Turner in asserting that the purpose of communal ritual is to compensate for the "conflicting principles of social organization which [. . .] underlie all society" (312).

18. Augustine's rejection of Manichaeism was a result of the dualism inherent in any pantheistic outlook. Dualism has a strong tendency toward amoral cosmology, fashioning Good and Evil as equal opposites beyond human morality. Augustine was motivated by a desire to affirm human morality and to metaphysically nullify evil by fashioning it as insubstantial. John Freccero describes the Augustinian solution to the problem of evil as hinging on the distinction between evil as an opposition and evil as a privation: "Evil was considered to be the absence of good, non-being, and therefore no positive thing" (191). Boethius also argues the insubstantiality of evil in the *Consolatio*. For dualism to fail, then, the idea of Nature as God had to be replaced by the idea of Nature as God's creation.

19. Life at Bertilak's castle, which mainly consists of the hunting and slaughtering of animals by Bertilak and the active pursuit of mating by Lady Bertilak, is more life-like than the silly, party-game atmosphere of Arthur's rather juvenile court. It is at Arthur's court, after all, that the decapitated Green Knight miraculously retrieves his head and informs Gawain to meet him in a year to receive the return stroke. At the Green Chapel Gawain receives a real but nonfatal blow from Bertilak, which is consistent with the life-like quality of the tale's mystical space in contrast with the festive quality of Camelot. When Gawain returns home he is distinctly uneasy in the naive gaiety of the Court. In the contrast between Arthur's and Bertilak's realms we can perceive the nominalist flavor of the late Medieval construction of the human experience, a view which carefully differentiates the unnerving and inscrutable mysteries of experience from the parlor game certainties of logic.

Bibliography

Aers, David. *Medieval Literature; Criticism, Ideology and History*. Brighton, UK: Harvester, 1986.

Andrew, Malcom and Ronald Waldron, eds. *The Poems of the Pearl Manuscript*. York Medieval Texts, second series. Berkeley: U of California P, 1978.

Ashley, Kathleen M. "Cultural Approaches to Medieval Drama." *Approaches to Teaching Medieval English Drama*. Ed. Richard K. Emmerson. New York: MLA, 1990. 57-66.

Auerbach, Erich. "Figura." *Scenes from the Drama of European Literature*. Trans. Ralph Manheim. New York: Meridian, 1959.

Augustine, of Hippo. *The City of God*. Trans. Marcus Dods. NY: Hafner, 1948.

Augustine, of Hippo. The *Confessions of St. Augustine*. Trans. Edward B. Pusey. New York: Modern Library, 1949.

Augustine, of Hippo. *On Christian Doctrine*. Trans. D. W. Robertson, Jr. New York: Liberal Arts, 1958.

Axton, Richard. *European Drama of the Early Middle Ages*. London: Hutchinson, 1974.

Beadle, Richard, ed. *The Cambridge Companion to Medieval English Theatre*. NY: Cambridge U P, 1994.

Beadle, Richard, ed. *The York Plays*. London: Edward Arnold, 1982.

Beadle, Richard and Pamela M. King, eds. *York Mystery Plays; A Selection in Modern Spelling*. Oxford: Clarendon, 1984.

Beckwith, Sarah. *Signifying God; Social Relation and Symbolic Act in the York Corpus Christi Plays*. Chicago: U of Chicago P, 2001.

Bethurum, Dorothy. *Critical Approaches to Medieval Literature*. New York: Columbia U P, 1960.

104

Bevington, David. *From Mankind to Marlowe; Growth of Structure in the Popular Drama of Tudor England.* Cambridge: Harvard U P, 1962.

Bevington, David. *Medieval Drama.* Boston: Houghton Mifflin, 1975.

Bevington, David. "Why Teach Medieval Drama?" *Approaches to Teaching Medieval English Drama.* Ed. Richard K. Emmerson. New York: MLA, 1990. 151-156.

Bloomfield, Morton W. "Symbolism in Medieval Literature." *Modern Philology* 56 (1958): 73-81.

Boethius. *The Consolation of Philosophy.* Trans. W. V. Cooper. New York: Random House, 1943.

Boethius. *De Consolatione Philosophiae.* Ed. Karl Buchner. Heidelberg: Carl Winter, 1960.

Boucher, Holly Wallace. "Nominalism: The Difference for Chaucer and Boccaccio." *Chaucer Review* 20 (1986): 213-220.

Briscoe, Marianne G. and John C. Coldewey, eds. *Contexts for Early English Drama.* Bloomington, IN: Indiana U P, 1989.

Burke, Kenneth. *A Rhetoric of Motives.* 1950. Berkeley: U of California P, 1969.

Butler, J. Donald. *Four Philosophies and their Practice in Education and Religion.* 3rd ed. New York: Harper & Row, 1968.

Carpenter, Nan Cooke. "Music in the *Secunda Pastorum.*" Speculum 26 (1951): 696-700.

Cawley, A. C., ed. *The Wakefield Pageants in the Towneley Cycle.* Manchester: Manchester U P, 1958.

Chaucer, Geoffrey. *The Complete Poetry and Prose of Geoffrey Chaucer.* Ed. John H. Fisher. New York: Holt, Rinehardt and Winston, 1977.

Clopper, Lawrence M. "Shifting Typologies in Langland's Theology of History" *Typology and English Medieval Literature.* Ed. Hugh T. Keenan. New York: AMS, 1992. 227-240.

Collier, Richard J. *Poetry and Drama in the York Corpus Christi Play.* Hamden, CT: Archon, 1978.

Collins, Patrick J. *The N-Town Plays and Medieval Picture Cycles.* Early Drama, Art, and Music Monograph Series 2. Kalamazoo, MI: Medieval Institute, 1979.

Collins, Patrick J. "Narrative Bible Cycles in Medieval Art and Drama." *The Drama of the Middle Ages; Comparative and Critical Essays.* Ed. Clifford Davidson, et. al. New York: AMS, 1982. 118-139.

Collins, Patrick J. "Typology, Criticism, and Medieval Drama." *Comparative Drama* 10 (1976-77): 298-313.

Coulton, G. G. *Studies in Medieval Thought.* New York: Russell & Russell, 1965.

Cox, John D. and David Scott Kastan, eds. *A New History of Early English Drama.* New York: Columbia U P, 1997.

Craig, Hardin. *English Religious Drama of the Middle Ages.* Oxford: Clarendon, 1955.

Cursor Mundi. Ed. Richard Morris. EETS o.s. 57, 59, 62, 68, 69. London, 1874-1892.

Davidson, Clifford. *From Creation to Doom; The York Cycle of Mystery Plays.* New York: AMS, 1984.

Davidson, Clifford. *Drama and Art; An Introduction to the Use of Evidence from the Visual Arts for the Study of Early Drama.* Early Drama, Art, and Music Monograph Series 1. Kalamazoo, MI: Medieval Institute, 1977.

Davidson, Clifford. *Gesture in Medieval Drama and Art.* Early Drama, Art, and Music Monograph Series 28. Kalamazoo, MI: Medieval Institute, 2001.

Davidson, Clifford. "Positional Symbolism and English Medieval Drama." *Comparative Drama* 25 (1991): 66-76.

Davidson, Clifford, C. J. Gianakaris and John H. Stroupe, eds. *The Drama of the Middle Ages; Comparative and Critical Essays.* New York: AMS, 1982.

de Grazia, Margreta. "World Picture, Modern Periods, and the Early Stage."
    A New History of Early English Drama. Ed. John D. Cox and David Scott
    Kastan. New York: Columbia U P, 1997. 7-21.

De Wulf, Maurice. *An Introduction to Scholastic Philosophy; Medieval and
    Modern*. Trans. P. Coffey. New York: Dover, 1956.

Delasanta, Rodney. "Nominalism and Typology in Chaucer." *Typology and
    English Medieval Literature*. Ed. Hugh T. Keenan. New York: AMS,
    1992. 121-140.

Diller, Hans-Jurgen. "The Craftsmanship of the Wakefield Master." *Medieval
    English Drama; Essays Critical and Contextual*. Ed. Jerome Taylor and
    Alan H. Nelson. Chicago: U of Chicago P, 1972. 245-259.

Diller, Hans-Jurgen. "Laughter in Medieval English Drama: A Critique of
    Modernizing and Historical Analysis." *Comparative Drama* 36 (2002):
    1-19.

Donaldson, E. Talbot. "Patristic Exegesis in the Criticism of Medieval Literature:
    The Opposition." *Critical Approaches to Medieval Literature*.
    Ed. Dorothy Bethurum. New York: Columbia U P, 1960. 1-26.

Douglas, Mary. "Cultural Bias." *In the Active Voice*. Boston: Routledge &
    Kegan Paul, 1982. 183-254.

Douglas, Mary. *Implicit Meanings; Essays in Anthropology*. Boston: Routledge
    & Kegan Paul, 1975.

Douglas, Mary. "Introduction to Grid/Group Analysis." *Essays in the Sociology
    of Perception*. Ed. Mary Douglas. Boston: Routledge & Kegan Paul,
    1982. 1-8.

Eco, Umberto and Constantino Marmo, eds. *On the Medieval Theory of Signs*.
    Foundations of Semiotics Vol 21. Philadelphia: John Benjamins, 1989.

Elliott, Jr., John R. "The Sacrifice of Isaac as Comedy and Tragedy." *Medieval
    English Drama; Essays Critical and Contextual*. Ed. Jerome Taylor and
    Alan H. Nelson. Chicago: U of Chicago P, 1972. 157-176.

Emmerson, Richard K. "Figura and the Medieval Typological Imagination."
    Typology and English Medieval Literature. Ed. Hugh T. Keenan.
    New York: AMS, 1992. 7-42.

Emmerson, Richard K., ed. *Approaches to Teaching Medieval English Drama.* New York: MLA, 1990.

Freccero, John. "Cosmology and Rhetoric." *Order and Disorder.* Ed. Paisley Livingston. Stanford Literature Studies 1. Saratoga, CA: ANMA Libri, 1984. 190-8.

Frye, Northrop. *Anatomy of Criticism.* Princeton, NJ: Princeton U P, 1957.

Gardiner, F. C. *The Pilgrimage of Desire.* Leiden: Brill, 1971.

Gash, Anthony. "Carnival Against Lent: The Ambivalence of Medieval Drama." *Medieval English Drama; Essays Critical and Contextual.* Ed. Jerome Taylor and Alan H. Nelson. Chicago: U of Chicago P, 1972. 74-98.

Gayley, Charles Mills. *Plays of Our Forefathers and Some of the Traditions upon Which They Were Founded.* 1907. Reprint. New York: Biblo and Tannen, 1968.

Geertz, Clifford. *Local Knowledge.* New York: Basic Books, 1983.

Gibson, Gail McMurray. *The Theater of Devotion: East Anglian Drama and Society in the Late Middle Ages.* Chicago: U of Chicago P, 1989.

Graham-White, Anthony. "'Ritual' in Contemporary Theatre and Criticism." *ETJ* 28 (1976): 318-324.

Greenblatt, Stephen. "Call for Action on Problems in Scholarly Book Publishing." Modern Language Association 17 July 2003. http://www.mla.org/rep_scholarly_pub

Hardison, O. B., Jr. *Chrisitian Rite and Christian Drama in the Middle Ages: Essays in the Origin and Early History of Modern Drama.* Baltimore: Johns Hopkins U P, 1965.

Healy, Sr. Emma Therese. *Saint Bonaventure's De Reductione Artium ad Theologiam; A Commentary with an Introduction and Translation.* St. Bonaventure, NY: St. Bonaventure U, 1955.

Homan, Richard L. "Ritual Aspects of the York Cycle." *Theatre Journal* 33 (1981): 303-315.

Jaspers, James M. "How the Research-University Model Has Killed the Creativity of Humanists and Social Scientists." *Chronicle Careers* 7 May 2002. http://chronicle.com/jobs/2002/02/2002020701c.htm.

Jensen, Minna Skafte. "The Homeric Epics and Greek Cultural Identitiy." *Religion, Myth, and Folklore; The Kalevala and its Predecessors.* Ed. Lauri Honko. Religion and Society 30. New York: Mouton de Gruyter, 1990. 29-48.

Johnston, Alexandra F. and Margaret [Dorrell] Rogerson, eds. *York*, Vol. 1. Records of Early English Drama. Toronto: U of Toronto P, 1979.

Kahrl, Stanley J. *Traditions of Medieval English Drama.* London: Hutchinson, 1974.

Kaske, R. E. "Patristic Exegesis in the Criticism of Medieval Literature: The Defense." *Critical Approaches to Medieval Literature.* Ed. Dorothy Bethurum. New York: Columbia U P, 1960. 27-60.

Keenan, Hugh T., ed. *Typology and English Medieval Literature.* New York: AMS, 1992.

Kevelson, Roberta. *Charles S. Peirce's Method of Methods.* Foundations of Semiotics Vol 17. Philadelphia: John Benjamins, 1987.

King, Pamela M. and Clifford Davidson, eds. *The Coventry Corpus Christi Plays.* Early Drama, Art, and Music Monograph Series 27. Kalamazoo, MI: Medieval Institute, 2000.

Knowles, David. *The Evolution of Medieval Thought.* New York: Random House, 1962.

Kolve, V. A. *The Play Called Corpus Christi.* Stanford, CA: Stanford U P, 1966.

Leigh, David J. "The Doomsday Mystery Play: An Eschatological Morality." *Medieval English Drama; Essays Critical and Contextual.* Ed. Jerome Taylor and Alan H. Nelson. Chicago: U of Chicago P, 1972. 260-278.

Livingston, Paisley, ed. *Order and Disorder.* Stanford Literature Studies 1. Saratoga, CA: ANMA Libri, 1984.

Lumiansky, R. M. and David Mills, eds. *The Chester Mystery Cycle.* 2 vols. London: Oxford UP for ETTS, 1974, 1986.

Manly, William M. "Shepherds and Prophets: Religious Unity in the Towneley *Secunda Pastorum*." *PMLA* 78 (1963): 151-155.

Meditations on the Life of Christ. Ed. and Trans. Isa Ragusa and Rosalie B. Green. Princeton, NJ: Princeton U P, 1961.

Meyers, Walter E. "Typology and the Audience of the English Cycle Plays." *Typology and English Medieval Literature*. Ed. Hugh T. Keenan. New York: AMS, 1992. 261-274.

The Middle English Harrowing of Hell and Gospel of Nicodemus. Ed. William H. Hulme. EETS e.s. 100. London, 1908.

Mills, David. *The Chester Mystery Cycle*. East Lansing, MI: Colleagues, 1992.

Mirk, John. *Festial: A Collection of Homilies*. Ed. Theodor Erbe. EETS e.s. 96. London, 1905.

Morgan, Margery. "'High Fraud': Paradox and Double-plot in the English Shepherd's Plays." *Speculum* 39 (1964): 676-89.

Muller, Herbert J. *Freedom in the Ancient World*. New York: Bantam, 1961.

Munson, William F. "Audience and Meaning in Two Medieval Dramatic Realisms." *The Drama of the Middle Ages; Comparative and Critical Essays*. Ed. Clifford Davidson, et. al. New York: AMS, 1982. 183-206.

Nelson, Alan H. "The Temptation of Christ; or, The Temptation of Satan." *Medieval English Drama; Essays Critical and Contextual*. Ed. Jerome Taylor and Alan H. Nelson. Chicago: U of Chicago P, 1972. 218-229.

Nelson, Alan H. "Some Configurations of Staging in Medieval English Drama." *Medieval English Drama; Essays Critical and Contextual*. Ed. Jerome Taylor and Alan H. Nelson. Chicago: U of Chicago P, 1972. 116-147.

Nissé, Ruth. "Staged Interpretations: Civic Rhetoric and Lollard Politics in the York Plays." *Journal of Medieval and Early Modern Studies* 28 (1998): 427-52.

The Northern Passion. Ed. Frances A. Foster. EETS o.s. 145,147. London, 1913, 1916.

Panofsky, Erwin. *Early Netherlandish Painting; Its Origins and Character*, Vol. 1. Cambridge, MA: Harvard U P, 1953.

Panofsky, Erwin. *Gothic Architecture and Scholasticism*. Cleveland: World, 1951.

Patterson, Lee. "Historical Criticism and the Claims of Humanism." *Chaucer to Spenser: A Critical Reader*. Ed. Derek Pearsall. Malden, MA: 1999. 246-279.

Peirce, Charles Sanders. *Writings of Charles S. Peirce; A Chronological Edition*, Vol. 2, 1867-1871. Ed. Edward C. Moore. Bloomington, IN: Indiana U P, 1982.

Poteet II, Daniel P. "Time, Eternity, and Dramatic Form in *Ludus Conventriae*." *The Drama of the Middle Ages; Comparative and Critical Essays*. Ed. Clifford Davidson, et. al. New York: AMS, 1982. 232-248.

Poulet, George. *Studies in Human Time*. Trans. Eliot Coleman. Baltimore: Johns Hopkins U P, 1956.

Riggio, Milla Cozart, ed. *The Play of Wisdom; Its Text and Contexts*. AMS Studies in the Middle Ages, No. 14. NY: AMS, 1998.

Robertson, D. W., Jr. *A Preface to Chaucer*. Princeton, NJ: Princeton U P, 1962.

Robertson, D. W., Jr. "'The Question of Typology' and the Wakefield *Mactacio Abel*." *Essays in Medieval Culture*. Princeton, NJ: Princeton U P, 1980. 218-232.

Robinson, J. W. "The Art of the York Realist." *Medieval English Drama; Essays Critical and Contextual*. Ed. Jerome Taylor and Alan H. Nelson. Chicago: U of Chicago P, 1972. 230-244.

Robinson, J. W. *Studies in Fifteenth-Century Stagecraft*. Kalamazoo, MI: Medieval Institute, 1991.

Roddy, K. P. "Epic Qualities in the Cycle Plays." *Medieval Drama*. Stratford-Upon-Avon Studies 16. London: Edward Arnold, 1973. 155-171.

Ross, Lawrence, J. "Symbol and Structure is the *Secunda Pastorum*." *Medieval English Drama; Essays Critical and Contextual*. Ed. Jerome Taylor and Alan H. Nelson. Chicago: U of Chicago P, 1972. 177-211.

Rossiter, A. P. *English Drama from Early Times to the Elizabethans*. London: Hutchinson, 1950.

Said, Edward. *The World, the Text and the Critic*. Cambridge, MA: Harvard U P, 1983.

Scholes, Robert. "The Evaluation of Faculty Members in the Culture of 'Excellence.'" *MLA Newsletter* 36.2 (2004): 3.

Sellers, Maud, ed. *York Memorandum Book A/Y*. Surtees Soc., 120, 125. Durham, UK. 1911, 1915.

Shakespeare, William. *The Complete Works of Shakespeare*. Ed. David Bevington. Updated 4th ed. New York: Longman, 1997.

Sheingorn, Pamela. "Typology and the Teaching of Medieval Drama." *Approaches to Teaching Medieval English Drama*. Ed. Richard K. Emmerson. New York: MLA, 1990. 90-100.

Smith, Lucy Toulmin, ed. *York Plays: the plays performed by the crafts or mysteries of York, on the day of Corpus Christi in the 14th, 15th, and 16th centuries*. EETS, 1885. Reprint. NY: Russell & Russell, 1963.

Stevens, Martin. *Four Middle English Mystery Cycles; Textual, Contextual, and Critical Interpretations*. Princeton, NJ: Princeton U P, 1987.

Stevens, Martin. "Medieval Drama: Genres, Misconceptions, and Approaches." *Approaches to Teaching Medieval English Drama*. Ed. Richard K. Emmerson. New York: MLA, 1990. 36-49.

Taylor, Jerome. "The Dramatic Structure of the Middle English Corpus Christi, or Cycle, Play." *Medieval English Drama; Essays Critical and Contextual*. Ed. Jerome Taylor and Alan H. Nelson. Chicago: U of Chicago P, 1972. 148-156.

Taylor, Jerome and Alan H. Nelson, eds. *Medieval English Drama; Essays Critical and Contextual*. Chicago: U of Chicago P, 1972.

Thoresby, John. *The Lay Folks' Catechism*. Ed. Thomas F. Simmons and Henry E. Nolloth. EETS o.s. 118. London, 1901.

Trapp, J. B., Douglas Gray, and Julia Boffey, eds. *Medieval English Literature*. 2nd ed. Oxford: Oxford U P, 2002.

Turner, Victor. *The Forest of Symbols*. Ithaca, NY: Cornell U P, 1967.

Turner, Victor. *The Ritual Process; Structure and Anti-Structure*. Ithaca, NY: Cornell U P, 1969.

William, of Ockham. *Philosophical Writings*. Ed. & Trans. Philotheus Boehner. Edinburgh: Nelson, 1957.

Williams, Arnold. "Typology and the Cycle Plays: Some Criteria." *Speculum* 43 (1969): 677-684.

Weissengruber, Erik Paul. "The Corpus Christi Procession in Medieval York: A Symbolic Struggle in Public Space." *Theatre Survey* 38 (1997): 117-137.

Woolf, Rosemary. *The English Mystery Plays*. Berkeley: U of California P, 1972.

Index

allegory (see also: anagoge, literal level, tropology, typology), ii, 6-9, 12, 14,17, 27, 29-31, 36, 51, 79-80, 98

anachronism, 27, 71, 73, 82, 88, 90-91, 93, 95

anagoge, ii, 9-10, 16-17, 26, 29, 36, 47, 51, 79-82, 84, 87-8

Arnold, Matthew, 11, 18-19

Ashley, Kathleen, 18, 23, 90, 92, 103

audience address, 85-8

Auerbach, Erich, 11, 13-17, 29-32, 34-5, 79, 91, 103

Augustine, of Hippo, *St.*, 19-20, 31-2, 34, 53-4, 64-5, 78, 101, 103

Axton, Richard, 94, 103

Beadle, Richard, iii, 41, 74, 97, 103

Beckwith, Sarah, 20, 24, 33, 103

Bevington, David, 17-18, 104, 111

Boethius, i, 9, 20, 29, 32, 34, 42-3, 45, 47, 65, 78, 84-5, 93, 98, 101, 104

Bible, *The*, 17, 20, 51, 58, 105;
Old Testament, 15-16, 21, 30-2, 34, 38-40, 55, 68, 94;
Genesis, 23-4; *Isaiah*, 68;
New Testament, 15-17, 30, 32, 34;
Matthew, 45-7, 58, 83; *Luke*, 84;
John, 24, 45; *I Corinthians*, 75;
Hebrews 94-95

Bonaventure, *St.*, 26, 51, 79, 107

Burke, Kennth, 2, 104

Butler, J. Donald, 97, 104

Carpenter, Nan Cooke, 88, 104

Chaucer, Geoffrey, 18, 99, 104, 106, 110

Clement V, *Pope - Decree of 1311*, ii, 88

Clopper, Lawrence M., 26, 104

Coventry plays, i, 108

Collier, Richard J., iii, 16, 21-7, 32, 36, 39-42, 52-53, 58, 65, 71, 76-7, 87-9, 94, 97-8, 105

Collins, Patrick J., 33-4, 105

cosmology, 2-12, 14, 18-24, 26-7, 29-35, 38-39, 42, 47, 49-50, 63-7, 69, 71, 75, 79, 81-2, 84, 90, 92, 95-6, 101, 106

Davidson, Clifford, iii, 16, 26, 32-3, 36, 40, 46-7, 54-5, 69-76, 97-9, 105, 108-110

de Grazia, Margreta, 3-4, 48, 106

De Wulf, Maurice, 66, 106

Diller, Hans-Jurgen, 8, 106

Donaldson, E. Talbot, 6, 106

Douglas, Mary, 1-5, 7-8, 14, 18, 20, 50, 77, 80-1, 98-100, 106

Duns Scotus, John, 5, 66

Eckhart, *Master*, 78

Emmerson, Richard K., 13-17, 29, 31-2, 51, 79, 103-4, 106-7, 111

epic poetry, 7, 92-3, 108, 110

epistemology, ii, 2-3, 7-10, 14, 16-17, 19-20, 27, 36-8, 43, 48-57, 62-67, 70-71, 73-5, 78, 80-2, 85-7, 90-7

Flemish (Netherlandish) painters, 10, 49, 64, 72-3, 109

Freccero, John, 101, 106

Frye, Northrop, 7, 107

Gardiner, F. C., 89, 107

Gash, Anthony, 8, 107

Gayley, Charles Mills, 68, 107

Gaytryge, Dan Jon, 53, 65, 87

Geertz, Clifford, 1-4, 6, 50, 99, 107
Gibson, Gail McMurray, 1, 107
Graham-White, Anthony, 91, 107
Greenblatt, Stephen, 5, 107
Healy, *Sr.* Emma Therese, 51-2, 98, 107
Homan, Richard L., 12, 20, 90-2, 100, 107
iconography, 12, 18, 23-5, 34, 36, 39, 46, 64, 70-3, 80, 82, 85-6, 99
idealism, 7, 66
Jaspers, James M., 4-7, 108
Jensen, Minna Skafte, 92-3, 108
Johnston, Alexandra, 97-8, 108
Kahrl, Stanley J., 52, 70-3, 108
Kaske, R. E., 6, 108
King, Pamela M., 42, 74, 103, 108
Kinghorn, A. M., 21-2
Knowles, David, 6, 54, 63, 65, 98-9, 108
Kolve, V. A., 16, 20, 32, 35, 37, 52-3, 55, 71-2, 77, 82, 90, 97-8, 108
Lactantius, 27, 70, 80-1, 85
literal level (allegory), ii, 9, 16-17, 26, 30, 51-2, 79-81, 86
liturgical drama, 36, 88-9, 94
Lollards, 8, 33, 83, 109
Malory, *Sir* Thomas, 96
Manly, William M., 6, 12-13, 19, 109
Meyers, Walter E., 6, 13-15, 19, 33, 97,109
Mercers (guild), 41, 91-2
Mirk, John, *Festial*, 19, 109
Morgan, Margery, 13-14, 109
Muller, Herbert J., 30-2, 65, 79, 109
Munson, William F., 89-90, 109
mysticism, 10, 16, 27, 49, 53-4, 63, 65, 78, 81-5, 88, 90, 93, 101
N-Town plays, 32-3, 35, 105
Nelson, Alan H., 35, 106-111
new historicism, 1, 3, 7, 50
Nicholas, of Cusa, 10, 49, 78

Nissé, Ruth, 33, 109
nominalism, ii, 5-6, 9-10, 20, 36-7, 49-50, 53, 63-71, 73, 75-8, 81-3, 86, 90, 98-9, 101, 104, 106
ontology, 38, 43, 51-52
Panofsky, Erwin, 63-4, 67, 72, 78, 81, 99, 109
Patterson, Lee, 3-4, 7-8, 110
Paul, *St.*, 30, 75, 94-5
Peirce, Charles Sanders, 5-6, 65-7, 108, 110
Poteet II, Daniel P. 36, 110
Poulet, George, 16, 110
pragmatism, 5, 65-67
realism, i, 49, 63, 65-78, 82, 85, 89, 94, 98-9, 109
revelation, 50-1, 58
ritual, 7, 10, 18-27, 30, 35, 67, 79, 81-96, 100, 107, 111-112
Roberston, Jr., D. W., 26-7, 32-3, 80, 99, 103, 110
Robinson, J. W., 56-7, 68, 73, 75-6, 85, 98, 110
Roddy, K. P., 7, 110
Rogerson, Margaret, 97-8, 108
Roscellinus, 65, 67, 99
Ross, Lawrence J., 13-14, 100, 110
Rossiter, A. P., 13-14, 52, 71, 110
Said, Edward, 19, 111
Scholes, Robert, 5, 111
Sellers, Maud, 91, 111
Shakespeare, William, 15, 23, 37, 97, 111
Sheingorn, Pamela, 12, 111
Sir Gawain and the Green Knight, 82, 101, 103
Stevens, Martin, 15, 18, 32, 36-7, 75, 95-6, 98, 111
Taylor, Jerome, 44, 106-111
theatrum mundi, 37, 88
Thomas Aquinas, *St.*, 63-4, 66, 78
Thoresby, John, *The Lay Folks' Catechism*, 98, 111

time, (concept of), i, 15-17, 27, 29,
    32, 34-6, 41-7, 84-5, 87, 89,
    93-4, 98, 110
tropology, ii, 9-10, 16-17, 26, 29,
    32-3, 50-2, 63, 79, 81
Turner, Victor, 23, 91, 100, 111-112
typology (allegorical), ii, 6, 8-9,
    11-17, 19-20, 26-7, 29-37, 39,
    41-2, 47-51, 67, 79-81, 91, 96,
    98, 104-106, 108-112
typology (modern sense), 2, 3, 6-7,
    67
Urban IV, *Pope - Papal Bull
    Transiturus of 1264*, ii, 88
verisimilitude, 10, 32-3, 72-3, 86, 99
Wakefield Master, 68, 85, 88, 106
Wakefield plays, 33, 68, 73, 85, 104,
    106, 110; *Annunciation play*, 33,
    Secunda Pastorum, 13, 88, 100,
    104, 108, 110
William, of Ockham, 5-6, 10, 49,
    63-7, 98-9, 112
Williams, Arnold, 12-14, 18, 80, 112
Weissengruber, Erik Paul, 7, 112
Woolf, Rosemary, 40, 112
York plays:
    I (Barkers), 20-4, 37, 39, 47;
    II (Plasterers), 20, 25, 37-9;
    III (Cardmakers), 38-9;
    IV (Fullers), 38-9;
    V (Coopers), 38-9;
    VI (Armorers) 38-9, 54-5;
    VII (Glovers), 38-9;
    VIII (Shipwrights), 39;
    IX (Fishers, Mariners), 39, 55;
    X (Parchmentmakers,
        Bookbinders), 39-40;
    XI (Hosiers), 39-40, 55-6;
    XII (Spicers), 17, 33, 40, 54;
    XIII (Pewterers, Founders), 40-1;
    XIV (Tilethatchers), 41, 56-7;
    XVII (Hatmakers, Masons,
        Laborers), 40;
    XVIII (Marshals), 57, 100;

XX (Spurriers, Lorimers), 74-5
XXIII (Curriers), 59-60, 81;
XXXI (Listers), 73-4;
XXXIII (Tilemakers), ii, 76;
XXXV (Pinners), 52;
XXXVI (Butchers), 58, 76-7;
XXXVII (Saddlers), 40, 98;
XXXIX (Winedrawers), 58, 86;
XL (Woolpackers), 60, 89;
XLI (Scriveners), 60, 86;
XLII (Tailors), 17, 41, 60;
XLIII (Potters), ii, 41, 58, 60-3;
XLIV (Drapers), 41;
XLV (Weavers), 41;
XLVI (Hostelers), 41, 44, 80;
XLVII (Mercers), ii, 41-7,
    83-84
York Realist, i, 49, 63, 68-75, 77, 85,
    98, 110